Point Blank

By Sam Hanna

This book is a work of non-fiction. Due to the sensitive nature of these events great care has been taken to avoid identifying the people involved with the incidents mentioned in this work. It is not the author's intent to embarrass or identify the people associated with these stories.

The Bible verses used in this book are from the following versions:

Holy Bible, New International Version®, NIV® Copyright ©1973, 1978, 1984, 2011 by Biblica, Inc.®

NET Bible® copyright ©1996-2006 by Biblical Studies Press, L.L.C.

New American Standard Bible (NASB)

Copyright © 1960, 1962, 1963, 1968, 1971, 1972, 1973, 1975, 1977, 1995 by The Lockman Foundation

Holy Bible. New Living Translation copyright© 1996, 2004, 2007, 2013 by Tyndale House Foundation.

The Holy Bible, English Standard Version Copyright © 2001 by Crossway Bibles

King James Version (KJV) by Public Domain

Table of Contents

Dedication

Acknowledgements

Foreword

Chapter 1	Let Your Spirit Be Known	1
Chapter 2	Love Your Enemies, Do Good to Them	15
Chapter 3	Greater Love Has No One Than This	21
Chapter 4	Who Hunger and Thirst for Justice	27
Chapter 5	With God All Things Are Possible	33
Chapter 6	Sowing Seeds	41
Chapter 7	It's a Job	55
Chapter 8	Oh, What a Tangled Web	69
Chapter 9	Facing the System	79
Chapter 10	The End of the Rope	87
Chapter 11	Iron Sharpens Iron	91
Chapter 12	Some Final Notes	101

This book is dedicated to Patrolman Mike McKain.

Mike was my friend and teacher. I think of him often. Mike took an interest in me and invested his time to make me a better police officer and a better man.

Thank You, Mike McKain.

Acknowledgements

There have been several people who have helped me and encouraged me throughout my career and life. They have believed in me and my vision

I first want to thank my wife Lori and children Kris, Matt, and Andrew for the sacrifices they made as I would get called out in the middle of family functions, called out during the night, and the times my mind was trying to make sense of a case I was working and not participating in family activities.

When I attended Eastside Church of God, Phil and Betty Fair became a big part of my life. They were like my second set of parents and Phil helped me to give my life to Christ. They are both gone now but I miss both of them.

Another aspect of my Christian experience was the time I was in the Fellowship of Christian Athletes (The God Squad). We traveled to churches from Indiana to Florida singing Christian songs and sharing our testimonies. Bob Blume was our leader and he and his wife Pat were great influences in my life and my Christian growth.

In my career as a police officer with the Madison County Sheriff's Department I give a lot of credit to Sheriff John Gunter. Another sheriff that helped my career was Scott Mellinger. We did not always see eye to eye on things, but I do believe he appreciated my work as an investigator and he encouraged me. Both John and Scott have been good friends and have influenced my growth as a police officer and a public servant.

I would also like to acknowledge Prosecutors William F. Lawler and Rodney Cummings. They both have supported me throughout the years and they hired an awesome staff. I could not have done what I did in my 38-year career with the Madison County Sheriff's Department without them and their staff.

I went to high school with Nick Vores. We rekindled our friendship approximately 13 years ago. He has always supported me in my adventures, my police career, and my growth as an individual. He offers advice and listens to my concerns.

I have become good friends with Alan Moore. He has supported me in my political, professional, and personal endeavors. He has always offered good advice and sometimes just listens as I talk about problems and come up with a solution.

I now work for The BlackWater Detective Agency. One of the owners, Joseph McKay, after interviewing me, hired me because of my resume. He also said he liked my giving spirit and compassionate heart. The fact he recognized this during our interview rejuvenated my spirit.

To all that I have mentioned above I want to say thank you. Your sacrifices, support, sharing of yourself, and just believing in me is, and always will be greatly appreciated. All of you have contributed to my work ethic, public servant heart, and most of all my Christian testimony.

Foreword

From Sheriff John Gunter:

During the 1970's I was working to build a professional agency in the Madison County Sheriff's office. To do this I needed good recruits.

I had worked for years with Jim Hanna, the father of Sam. When Sam was fresh out of college he came to me. Sam passed the required tests. He went off to the Indiana Law Enforcement Academy. He worked for me the last five years I was the Sheriff of the Madison County Sheriff's department.

In 1978, while I was attending the Sheriff's State Convention, an announcement was made that Sam had been shot. I jumped in my car and I set some kind of record getting back to Madison County. Thankfully Sam survived.

John Gunter Madison County Sheriff.

* * * * * *

From Major Dennis Maxey

I worked with Sam for 28 years at the department and had the opportunity to work several cases with him. Sam was always that "go to" Investigator. The person you wanted on the case when $1,000 of property was at stake or a very bad person was loose and needed to be locked up before another crime could be committed.

Sam prided himself on leaving no stone left unturned. As an investigator he would sometimes amaze me at his ability to sift through the important and not so important statements made by defendants. Sam was the type of Officer that never said "I can't" or "no." He was available 24 hours a day 7 days a week for any call out and would not cease until the job was completed.

Sam also had a lighter side. He was always able to not only take a joke, but also to give one back on occasion. He had the ability to balance his work, his family, and his faith. More than once I have told people if anyone ever breaks into my house I want Sam working the case because he will get your property back. He did this time and time again not only with property, but with getting the bad guys off the street. These are the guys who had hurt people and would hurt more people if left on the loose.

I was Major in 1998 and in charge of Investigations. Sam was a seasoned detective and begged for the harder to solve cases. He never said "It can't be done," or "I'll give you a number to call" when you needed help, but making that call and getting that information to the right people

Sam has been such an asset to the people of Madison County and the Madison County Police Department. He has received several crime buster awards and awards from several Sheriffs over his career. He has helped so many people, and to this date people walk up to him and thank him for the work he has done.

I am proud to call Sam my friend, my colleague, and have told my wife many times if I could have been half the Policeman Sam has been my career would have been complete.

Major Dennis Maxey Administrative Assistant and Interim Sheriff

* * * * * *

From Don McAllister:

When Sam Hanna asked me to help him write this book I wasn't sure about the project. While I had mastered the art of being the world's most unknown bestselling author with my novels *Angel and the Ivory Tower, The Pencil Man, The Art of Freezing Pickles,* and *Satchel at the Second Chance,* I had yet to work with a non-fiction piece. After hearing Sam's story I knew it had to be told.

Let me be clear; I did not write this book. The words are Sam Hanna's. I was the guy who structured the book for publication and that was about it. In a very real sense Sam mentored me while I was mentoring him.

This is a hard book to read at times. The stories are deeply moving as it touches on the deepest failures and sometimes the greatest successes of the human condition. As Sam passed on to me the sections of the book, I was at times deeply saddened. Other times I was thrilled at the high notes. It is clear that Sam honed his skills and made a lasting impression on the lives of the people he encountered.

It was an honor serving with Sam on this project. To find out how deep of an honor that was – READ THE BOOK.

Don McAllister, a write good fellow

Chapter 1

Let Your Spirit Be Known

Let your gentle spirit be known to all men. The Lord is near. Be anxious for nothing, but in everything by prayer and supplication with thanksgiving let your requests be made known to God. And the peace of God, which surpasses all comprehension, will guard your hearts and your minds in Christ Jesus. – Philippians 4:5-7 (NASB)

When the funeral is over and people speak of how they knew you, they will not say much about your wealth, or your trophies, or about the stuff you valued. They will talk about your spirit. Whether you were a rotten so-and-so or a saint, they will speak of how they felt when they crossed your path. The real winners in life are the ones who can inspire others to be better than they were naturally born to be.

My grandmother was one of those people. Her name was Anna, but we called her Sitto (sit too), which is Syrian for grandmother. Sitto came over on the boat from Syria by herself when she was 15-years-old. She raised ten children, again by herself, after my grandfather passed away.

To get by, she ran a small storefront grocery store. All the children would help to run the store as they got older. As my aunts and uncles started college or jobs they helped with home expenses and the younger children's schooling expenses.

She made sure that her children, as they got married, would come home for Sunday dinner. She was very religious. When she could not attend church the priest would come to her house to bless her and her family and to pray with her. Whenever you asked her a question she would answer it with a Bible verse.

Sitto was also emphatic when it came to respecting people of other races. It didn't matter to her if a person was white, black, red, or green. She treated everyone as God's children. I learned this from her and followed her example. I remember one of my first close interactions with an African-American. Woody Moore

1

was one of my football coaches and a true gentleman. What a fool I would have been if I had rejected him because of his race.

Woody went to Frisch's (a popular Anderson, Indiana restaurant) one night to ask my dad if I could work for the Urban League in the summer between my junior and senior year in high school. There were eleven African-American students and myself that worked together all summer. During this job one of my coworkers hit me on my upper lip by accident. He thought I was mad and wanted to fight him, but I told him it was my fault because I was not paying attention. We shook hands and then went to get my lip stitched up. We were all God's children and treated each other as God treated us. Sitto taught me this through her actions. I can think of many wonderful friendships I would have missed if I hadn't heeded her example.

Sitto taught me to respect and obey my mother and father, and the importance of family. She insisted that the whole family get together at least once a year. When we were all with her she said she was happy. When we would leave Pennsylvania to return home she would bless our car for a safe trip.

I am not Sitto. I didn't experience the hardships of her life firsthand, but I am who I am because of the influence of her spirit.

My dad was a police officer for the city of Anderson for 23 years. He also worked part time as a security officer for Frisch's. I have been told by many men that, if it had not been for Dad, they may have ended up in the juvenile center or prison.

While working at Frisch's, Dad would see someone he thought had been involved in stealing something. He would tell them that he worked until 2 am. He wanted the stolen stuff in his car before he left to go home. I was told the kids called Dad "Banana Nose" because Dad had a large nose but they really respected him. I was told that my dad would get on someone and make them pour the beer on the ground. Then, as he walked away, Dad would wink at them.

My father never talked to me about going into police work. When I decided to do so, he told me to always be fair and honest.

2

Let Your Spirit Be Known

I am not my dad. I didn't directly experience everything he experienced in life, but I am who I am because of the influence of his spirit. I was certainly a better police officer because of his advice and his example.

My mom was not an educated lady, but she was smart. She worked for Culligan soft water as a bookkeeper, then as a saleslady. She could do anything from wallpapering a room to upholstering furniture. She was my Cub Scout leader and the Girl Scout leader for my sisters. She always told me that she believed in me and that I would make difference in people's lives someday.

My parents were married for 50 years before Mom died. People often told me that they would see my mom and dad in a car and she would be sitting right next to him.

When I became a police officer my mom and dad were very supportive. They let me make my own decisions then supported me. We were not rich people but our parents made sure our needs were met and told us to be proud to be a Hanna.

I am not my mom. I did not walk every step of her life with her. I didn't feel the pain of her labor or her frustration when she balanced the needs of her job, her husband, and her children. What I did get from my mom was her love and her gentle spirit. The spirit of my mother has made me a better man.

I was very fortunate to have such a foundation. My parents and Sitto gave me love and security. They taught me their good character through their words and deeds and they expected me to follow their teachings. In my line of work I've seen the damage done to people by parents who were abusive, neglectful, or just poor examples to their children.

Fortunately there are also outside mentors who can help fill that gap and build character in those who can't get that foundation at home. I've tried to be that kind of example in my police work. I'll detail some of that later.

Dad and I both played football for Anderson College. My football career started at Riley elementary school, where I played for George Harris.

Let Your Spirit Be Known

I was not very big and did not start. We were playing one game and the opponent's team had an unstoppable fullback. During the game Coach Harris asked who could stop the fullback. I said I would. This action was out of character for me.

I was put on the defensive line as nose tackle. The first time I tackled him I held on like my life depended on it. I stopped him all night. We lost the game, but I won my battle.

Coach Harris made me realize that I could do anything I set my mind to.

I then played 8th grade football for Nate Johnson at Central Junior High School. Mr. Johnson was a soft-spoken man, but he helped me to realize that you can reach your dream by putting forth the effort to improve each day. He had played football for Anderson College and was an excellent running back. He showed us videos of when he played. Every time he had the ball he ran like he was determined to run for a touchdown.

Coach Johnson had also tried out for the Olympics. He was a sprinter. I had never seen anyone run that fast. This inspired me to play high school football even though I was not that big.

The desire to play also led me to become a better student. I worked on my grades to stay eligible to play sports. The discipline I learned as an athlete carried over to the classroom.

Coach Johnson taught me that raw talent wasn't enough. I had to push myself to develop that talent. How many talented athletes go on to the professional ranks and then blow their chance by letting their press releases go to their heads?

I was always polite and courteous. When I added Coach Johnson's lessons on discipline and drive, I became a better player and a better young man.

I played 9th grade football for Central Junior High School. George Harris was again my football coach. He made sure everyone played in the game. He taught the fundamentals of the game so we were competitive. I was always impressed with Mr. Harris because no matter how big or small you were, talented or not, he always had praise for your individual performance.

I learned that everyone falls short from time to time and that everyone has a moment when they shine. That would later be a valuable tool in my belt when I went into police work.

Pat King and Don Brandon were my 10th grade football coaches. They demanded perfection.

They broke us up into two squads. The squad that had the better week in practice started the next game. This inspired me to not only compete with my teammates, but with myself as well. I learned that if I worked hard and improved I could earn the reward of starting the next game.

Coach King and Coach Brandon were great motivators. They taught me that I could make my own world better if I took the time to encourage others.

In my junior and senior years at Anderson High School, I played for Pete Russo, Woody Moore, and Phil Sullivan. Every summer, before the season began, the players had conditioning practices and no coaches were allowed. We practiced at Northside Junior High School. We could see Pete Russo watching from afar using binoculars. Afterwards he would come over and talk to us. He kept telling me not to come out and that I would never play for him. I went to pick up equipment and he told me to go home before I got hurt. When I went to practice there were position rosters on the board. I was always listed at the bottom of the guards.

Some people might think that Coach Russo's methods were cruel and discouraging. It made me push all the harder to make the team. I now know that he wouldn't have said those things if he hadn't seen that potential in me.

We had practiced two weeks and I went in one day and could not find my gear. I went to talk to Mr. Russo. He said. "Son, your equipment is in your locker." He then showed me where all the starter's equipment was housed in a larger screened locker room. I was the only junior on the starting line. The rest were seniors.

Pete Russo had a way of challenging and motivating you on your own level. I started for the Anderson Indians football team in both my junior and senior years. I earned an honorary mention in the conference both years.

Coach Russo taught me that life isn't fair. You have to face the challenges head on and earn your place.

After I graduated from Anderson High School I decided not to go to college. The Anderson City Police Department had a cadet program and I decided I would do this until I was 21 then join the force.

The football season had already started when I received a phone call from my friend Dave Braittain who was the team manager for the Anderson College Ravens. He told me that Don Brandon wanted to talk to me.

Don, who had been my 10th grade football coach, was now the line coach for the Ravens. Coach Brandon got on the phone and asked if I had ever thought about college. I said at one time I did want to go, but I had decided against it. Coach Brandon asked me to come play football at Anderson College. I said I was not in shape, other than I had been lifting weights, and I had no money. He told me to go talk to H.L. Baker at Anderson College. He helped me to get college loans and grants through the work study program.

The next day I was at football practice. I was a couple weeks behind everyone else. We did the hamburger drill. After practice my stomach was hurting, I threw up, and had trouble breathing. As I walked off the field, Dick Young put his hand on me and said I will get in shape because it was evident I had played for Pete Russo. He said I had good technique.

I played my first year on a few specialty teams. Then I got overconfident and, when we went to the Nationals, Coach Brandon took me out. That challenged me to never let up again. I started as an offensive pulling guard the next three years. I made Honorable Mention NAIA Division 2 my senior year. I was an okay player but a very determined one.

I had learned that a college education was within my reach and that I was a better man for having tried. I learned that confidence and discipline were good tools to keep in the belt, but that overconfidence would keep me out of the game of life.

Coach Harris taught me to take on new challenges.

Coach Johnson taught me that raw talent wasn't enough, and that I had to train and improve myself.

Coach King and Coach Brandon had taught me the value of motivating others. Coach Brandon would later teach me to keep my value in perspective, and to be humble in my achievements least I lose that perspective.

Coach Russo taught me that life isn't fair, but that you can make it work if you are willing to put in the effort.

As an adult I took a hand at coaching both little league baseball, and football in the Anderson Community Schools. I felt an obligation to pass on what I had learned from my coaches. Sometimes it was the players who taught me.

I coached baseball throughout the years that my three sons were in little league. During this time I made sure that everyone played.

One year, at the Franklin little league, we started on a day that was cold with blowing light snow flurries. We started the day out by taking individual and team pictures. One little five-year-old boy refused to get his picture taken. I was able to convince him to get his team picture taken by kneeling down in front of him and putting my arm around him. I told him his grandmother would love to have his picture on her television set. I learned to talk to the young children on their level.

A few years later I coached a 10-year-old boy in minor league. He was a left-hander and was awkward. I played him one game in right field. We lost the game but I considered it a victory because he caught a fly ball for an out. I took everyone to Dairy Queen to celebrate. It was like that game where Coach Harris had put me in against that unstoppable fullback. It was that young boy's chance to try something that was outside of his comfort zone and he played well.

Several years later I drafted a young man to play on my team. He should have played in the majors, but was told the coaches

7

didn't want to deal with his father. I took him on my team. He was an awesome pitcher and catcher and always the first one to practice and the last to leave.

On Election Day that year he did not show up. No one had seen him, so after practice I went by his house. I was told he had been involved in a mishap earlier in the day that left him with major burns over most of his body. The next day I went to the Riley Hospital burn unit to see the boy. We talked, and I promised him he would play at least one game before the end of the season. He did in fact play our last game in right field. We lost the game but the young man won by playing – and in my mind that was huge.

Coaching little league is not about winning games. It's about building character. We help the players reach their individual goals and not just how to win a plaque.

I have also been a coach for junior high and high school football. In 1977 I coached 9th grade football at Anderson High School. My better players got moved up to reserve and varsity squads by the varsity coach. We played the season with a small squad and lost more games than we won. I decided to teach fundamentals and help the players identify their strong and weak points to the position they wanted to play. I wanted to help prepare them for the next three years of high school. One of my players became a State Trooper, one became a fireman, another became a news reporter, and one now owns his own business. That was the score I kept in my won/loss column.

In the late years of the 1970s I coached at Highland High School with Dave Edwards who I had played for in college. I tried to treat each player as I did the others I had coached. Unfortunately I later ended up arresting two of my Highland players for burglary. Another was arrested by two other county officers during football season for burglary. This player was later up for most valuable player and captain of the team. Because he was not truthful he lost the honors. I respected that decision because again as coaches we try to build character. He later grew up and became a pilot. He is an awesome young man who learned from his mistakes.

8

Let Your Spirit Be Known

A few years after coaching at Highland I coached 8th grade football at Northside Middle School with Robert (Buckie) Bookhart. We tried to teach the players that if you misbehave in school you would not start games and may not play at all if the offense was really bad.

I coached my last two years at Eastside Middle School as head coach. It was a really good team that won every game except two in two years.

At one of the practices my very best player took a cheap shot at one of his teammates. I was told they had a disagreement earlier in the day. The player was held accountable and the other members of the team were shocked that I would come down hard on a star player. I made a clear impression on the others that that type of play would not be tolerated.

In my 38 years of law enforcement I have seen young men and women make poor choices. As a coach I felt it was my responsibility to not so much win games as to teach our future leaders a good work ethic, sportsmanship, good character, and better decision making. Winning games was all well and good, but learning how to play well and reduce your mistakes was a more important lesson for me. In law enforcement I saw too many people make a mistake in 30 seconds that would ruin the rest of their life.

My choice to go into law enforcement was influenced by yet another group of mentors. In the late 1960s I was in my last two years of high school. I weighed about 165 pounds while playing on the line on the Anderson High School football team. To improve my game my dad asked me to workout with weights with Mike McKinley and John Connell. They were both cadets on the Anderson City Police Department.

I initially had no idea what I was going to do after high school. Every time I worked out with Mike and John I heard them talk about being a Cadet with the city police department. They had started in the records department copying files onto microfilm. Before they were 21 they actually worked in the juvenile division.

They were sent into bars and liquor stores to see if they would be served, even though they were underage.

This job intrigued me. I thought how cool it would be to do this kind of police work until I was 21-years-old, and to join the uniformed police force and work where my dad worked.

I worked out almost daily lifting weights with Mike and John. If they were not available, I worked out with Randy Davis and Jack Fulda who were both police officers. I learned from all of them that the harder you worked the more you improved. It is because of these men that I weighed close to 200 lbs and had added 40lbs of muscle mass when I was called to play football for Anderson College. I was strong enough to compete on a college level. God used my interest in being a police cadet and weight lifting to prepare me for the next step.

God gave me these mentors not just to bulk up, but to put purpose in my young life. I had a much clearer idea now of what I wanted to be in my adult life and had added some valuable experience to get me there.

The leaders of the cadet program were there to help me to reach the finish line and fulfill God's plan for my life.

I was incredibly blessed as a young man to have these mentors in my life – these spirits, if you will, who had shaped my maturing spirit. However, the Bible speaks of the fruit of the spirit. No matter how gentle, or honest, or well intentioned our spirits might be, our good character is useless until we put it to work. Here are some examples of where I had the opportunity to take the gifts that were given to me and to put them into action.

In my law enforcement career I had two basic types of calls – responding to a possible crime or responding to an accident. An officer could have some idea of what to expect when responding to a crime – after all, a crime is usually something that follows a pattern. A traffic accident, by its very nature is chaotic and unpredictable. Most of the time we responded to fender benders and we filled out our reports. It was sad to know that someone would have to go through all the trouble of repairing their vehicle, but it wasn't tragic. Then there were the bad ones – the ones that broke your heart and required full use of that "gentle spirit."

* * * * * *

It was Christmas Day, 1975. I had been on the road for approximately two months. I was at my parents' home eating Christmas dinner. I had told my captain, Dick Whetsel, that I would take the on-call responses as I was not married and had to work at 4:00 p.m. anyway. It made sense to me that the officers with families should spend the day home.

Randy Simmons, a jail officer, was working day shift patrol. I heard on my portable radio that he had been sent to a fatal accident in northern Madison County. He was the only officer on the road.

I had to cut short my Christmas dinner with my parents to respond to a possible fatal accident at State Road 32 and county road 600 West. When I arrived I found a young man behind the wheel of a Volkswagen. He was deceased. A crowd was forming and several people said that they were family members of the young man. I had the sad duty of telling them that he was gone and I called for the coroner and back up officers to help with traffic control.

One of the family members then asked about their mother. They had just celebrated Christmas together and their son was taking her home. I looked in the passenger side of the Volkswagen and did not see her. I then pulled back clothes that had fallen forward against the smashed front seat. I pulled the seat back and my heart sank. I found the young man's grandmother deceased on the floorboard of the passenger side.

I took a deep breath and asked God to give me the right words to say to the family. They not only lost one, but two family members on Christmas Day leaving a family get together. I had never had to do this before, but I remembered that Sheriff John Gunter had once said to talk to victims of tragedies as if you are talking to your own family.

God gave me the words to say. I started by hugging the family and telling them what had happened. I ended the conversation with a hug.

Let Your Spirit Be Known

It was hard telling the family, but, as Sheriff Gunter had said, I treated the family with dignity, respect, and God's love. I have not forgotten this in 38 years with the Sheriff's department. Sheriff John Gunter is a Godly man who shared this love with me, making me a better police officer and man.

* * * * * *

There was another incident where I had to use that "gentle spirit" – this time with much more pleasant results.

My wife Lori had just had my youngest son Andrew. It was one of those times when the toughest of guys becomes tenderhearted and appreciative of the blessings of his wife and his children. Lori was still in Community Hospital. I had been in Alexandria, Indiana working a case. I was on my way back to Anderson to go see Lori and Andrew when I heard an accident dispatched on county road 900 North in the area of county road 200 East. I was close and proceeded to the location.

There had been five juveniles in the car – two in the front seat and three in the back seat. One of the girls in the back seat had been babysitting with the young toddler who was in the middle of back seat. The car hit a telephone pole and the toddler had been catapulted through the windshield.

The child was transported to Community Hospital. I went to the emergency room to see how the child was. She had been bleeding in numerous areas. The child's mom arrived at the hospital and was told that her daughter needed stitches. The girl's mom is a wonderful mother and she was very upset.

The mom had been asked to hold her child while the wounds were stitched up. She was too upset to do this so I volunteered to hold her. The little girl received around 100 stitches. While it hurt to see her in so much pain, it was also a real heart-tugger to hold this fragile life in my hands as the physicians did their work.

The little girl was a trooper. Her mom was very kind and supportive. She was released from the hospital to go home.

I then went to see my wife and my son. All the time I thought of how that little girl could have been one of my sons. I would hope that someone one would allow God to use them as God had just used me to comfort a child and her mom if this should ever happen to my family.

The next night I went to the little girl's home and checked on her. I spoke with her mom and watched the little girl play. As I left I gave the little girl a stuffed teddy bear. I was online a couple years ago and the little girl, now in her twenties, contacted me on Facebook. She identified who she was and showed me a photo. She had kept the stuffed teddy bear.

* * * * * *

It wasn't the badge, or the gun, or the vest that got me through these difficult times. It wasn't the weight training or the tough exterior that made me able to handle these incidents. It was that "gentle spirit" that I had learned from others before me that made the difference. I was a better man – a better officer – because I let that spirit be known.

Let Your Spirit Be Known

Chapter 2

Love Your Enemies, Do Good to Them

But love your enemies, do good to them, and lend to them without expecting to get anything back. Then your reward will be great, and you will be children of the Most High, because he is kind to the ungrateful and wicked. – Luke 6:35 (NIV)

Let's face it – it's easy to say that bad guys are bad guys and that they deserve what they get. While this is true, it is also important to realize that people do bad things, and we have to separate the act from the person. Even the worst of society are guaranteed a fair trial and proper treatment in this country. If a law enforcement officer loses sight of the fact that the person in his custody is also a human being, as well as a criminal, he will lose control of the game.

One good example comes from a simple act of feeding a hungry prisoner.

From the time I started my career in law enforcement until I retired I knew that when I left for work I may not come home. I was an aggressive police officer and took any challenge set before me very seriously. I took precautions, but was never afraid to do my job.

I tried to treat everyone that came into my path fairly, and this is how God preserved my life. I remember the day I was transporting a prisoner back to the Madison County jail from Michigan City. It was around lunch time and I went through a McDonald's fast food drive through.

I bought each of us a hamburger, fries, and a Coke. He was handcuffed next to me so I had to hand feed him his lunch. He thanked me. I took him to the jail and had him booked in for court.

The same prisoner was transported by another officer sometime later. During the trip the prisoner spit a handcuff key from his mouth into his hand and took his cuffs off. He took the officer's gun and forced the officer to pull off to the side of the road. Then

15

he made him undress, took his police car, and left the officer in the field.

The prisoner was eventually caught by authorities in the Kokomo, Indiana area. I later saw this inmate at the Madison County jail. He told me that, when I transported him, he had planned to escape from me, but he said that I was nice to him and treated him like a human being, so he swallowed the key while I was hand feeding him.

God's right hand delivered me that day. He had taught me how to be kind to others and to pay attention to the needs of others. My life was preserved.

* * * * * *

The act of my keeping a level of fair play and common respect has led to some powerful testimonials from people who have said that my actions have made a positive difference in their life. In the following case it literally saved my life.

Sometimes compassion and the law seem to be in conflict. I arrested a woman one time whose step daughter had died in the front yard of her trailer after puncturing her jugular vein. The three year old child had fallen on a jagged piece of glass while her step mother slept on the couch in the trailer. The prosecutor had helped me to get a search warrant to go back to the trailer and take more pictures and measurements. When we got there the woman's husband and father of the dead child came to the front door with a shotgun.

He first told me and the other officers to get off his property. I told him we had a warrant and if he interfered he would go to jail. He then pointed the gun in my direction and said I was not allowed on his property but the other officers could do what they needed to do. I had every right to arrest him, and some might think to shoot him if he didn't drop his weapon. After all, he had a shotgun pointed at me. How was I to know if and when he might pull the trigger? It was obvious that he was in a distressed emotional state from losing his daughter, and I had arrested the stepmom. Instead of taking the tough guy approach I stood there and allowed him to focus on me until the job was done and we left.

I was later asked by one of the officers with me why I let the man intimidate me. I said I was not intimidated. I showed him compassion. Compassion was my weapon. Years ago, in an unrelated incident, he had been shot by a neighbor. Now he was dealing with losing his daughter and having his wife arrested for neglect. Yes, he had pointed a gun at me, but no one was hurt and that was all that mattered.

* * * * * *

I have always worked well with other police agencies. Captain Randy Simmons calls me a policeman's policeman. I was contacted by an Indiana State Police Investigator and asked if I could keep a man they had in custody busy. I was told that he and other officers from the state police had been working with the FBI on a stolen interstate commerce sting operation.

This suspect kept showing up with stolen property. I asked for information and was told that he had a stolen car at his house. I went to a park across from where he lived and watched for the stolen car to be driven off. After watching the residence for a day and a half I saw the suspect drive it from his residence.

I had a uniform officer stop him. He was arrested for possession of the stolen car. As I drove him to jail I talked with him about the choices he had made and encouraged him to do better.

He was in and out of jail faster than I could get the paperwork started on his arrest. I filed the charges. I did not hear anything about this man for awhile.

I was then contacted by the state police investigators. I was told that the man under suspicion had been arrested under his brother's name in Ohio. They said they were going to leave him there until the sting operation was over. I was also told that the suspect had been calling a fence and was trying to make a deal with him to get him out of jail.

I was contacted a third time by the state police. They told me that the suspect had been identified and was going to make bail. I put together two burglary cases. I had this man rearrested on the new charges and extradited back to the Madison County jail.

We had a pretrial conference with the suspect, his attorney, the deputy prosecutor handling the case, and myself. The man's attorney said his client would take four years in prison. I said the only thing that was going to happen was that he going to prison for 20 plus years because of his present and past criminal record.

Under Criminal Rule 4 the suspect was released from jail awaiting trial. A short time after he was released from jail I received a phone call from the Madison County Police department dispatcher. My family and I were getting ready to leave our house.

I answered the phone and was told there was a man on the other line who wanted to talk to the guy that "had been shot in the face." I spoke with him. He said he did not like me but respected the job I did. He told me he had been hired to put a bomb in my car.

I was floored. Why would anyone warn the person they were hired to kill? I wondered what I had done to earn the professional respect of this hit man. It was a real act of grace and protection – the kind of grace your wife prays for as she kisses you goodbye for the start of each watch.

The caller and I agreed to meet the next morning in Pendleton, Indiana.

I called Captain Randy Simmons and the State Police investigator I had been working with. The next morning I put together a picture line up to help identify who wanted me killed. Captain Simmons and I were running late to meet the man that had called me. Our dispatcher radioed me saying the man we were to meet wanted to know if I was going to meet him.

I chuckled and said to Simmons he must either be telling the truth or he really was going to kill me. We arrived at the prearranged location. Captain Simmons showed the man the line up, and he identified the suspect I've just mentioned as the man who wanted me killed. He said the man had told him I was standing in the way of him getting a plea agreement.

We then went to the State Police post. He called the man who had hired him to kill me and set up a marijuana buy. We had taped it and the suspect even talked about killing me on the tape. We contacted Sheriff Scott Mellinger. We advised him of what was going on and asked for money to make the drug buy.

The marijuana deal went down a couple days later. I heard again on tape how the man had hired this man to kill me. Sheriff Mellinger offered to put my family and I up at a motel until this was over.

I decided to stay home and trust God. Getting the initial phone call was already a miracle. I put this whole thing into God's hands.

My wife, Lori put it in perspective with an incident with my mom. My mom knew how to worry and, as you can imagine, she was really concerned about this situation. She came over to the house one day during this ordeal and saw Lori painting the garage door. She asked Lori if she should be out in front of the house painting the garage door, as she stood there wringing her hands.

Lori told her that she wasn't going to do anything stupid. The boys were no longer allowed to play in the front yard, but Lori refused to live in fear citing that "When you live in fear the devil wins." Mom said a reluctant "okay."

Sure, Lori may have been taking a risk, but, hey, "The door needed to be painted." Looking back on it Lori did note that it was sweet that Mom cared enough to say something.

The man that had been hired to kill me introduced an undercover ATF agent to the suspect. They met at a motel in Anderson, Indiana with the undercover agent. He had C-4 explosives and was carrying a revolver. Everything going on in the room was being taped and could be seen on a TV screen in the room where ATF agent James Quearry and I were watching.

We saw the undercover agent defuse the C-4 and neutralize it with a dummy fuse. He also showed us that the man who wanted me killed was carrying a gun.

As the suspect left the room he was met with several shotguns and handguns pointing at him. He was told to lay face down on the ground where the bomb and gun were taken from him. Sheriff Mellinger then told me to read the suspect his Miranda Rights. That was a good moment.

The arrest was made without incident. He was charged federally and received a 30 year sentence.

A second man was arrested for providing the bomb that was supposed to be used to kill me. The plan was to put the bomb in my car. The ATF agents said there was enough C-4 to blow up the entire block where I lived.

What upset me was the fact that I drove my kids to the bus stop every morning before work. I am an aggressive police officer but this plot put my children and neighbors in harm's way. That principled hit man's call had saved not only me, but countless other innocent lives.

God protected my family and our neighborhood. I thanked God after everything was done that no one was hurt – including the man who wanted me murdered.

Chapter 3

Greater Love Has No One Than This

Greater love has no one than this: to lay down one's life for one's friends. – John 15:13 (NIV)

This is a commandment that is usually thought of in connection with a righteous person. It fits perfectly with the crucifixion of our lord Jesus. God has shown me that there are imperfect men who also deserve our honor and praise. While I loathe the crimes that people commit, I've been able to separate those crimes from the people God made. This respect for the person has saved my life on at least one occasion. You might consider Jackie Martin an unlikely hero, but he is one in my book.

Several months prior to December 18, 1993 Jackie Martin, and three other men, came to Madison County where they committed approximately six burglaries and stole two trucks. Later on that Friday afternoon one of the trucks was located in Crawfordsville, Indiana. I made arrangements to have the truck locked up.

On Monday morning I drove to Crawfordsville and processed the truck. I lifted several finger prints. I then went to the Sheriff's department and the police department and requested prints of known burglars and car thieves.

I took the lifted impressions and the known latent finger prints back to Madison County. Randy Simmons was the supervisor over the investigation division and a fingerprint expert. He compared the prints and matched one young man that lived in the Crawfordsville area. I investigated him, Jackie Martin and two brothers. I ended up arresting all four for burglaries and auto theft.

Jackie Martin cooperated in the investigation. Sheriff Dennis Rice who had assisted me in the investigation asked if they could use Jackie Martin as an informant. He said that the two brothers were part of crime family another officer had been working.

Jackie agreed to do so. He made numerous drug buys and gave information on other things. After arrests were made we started hearing threats in Crawfordsville against Jackie Martin and me.

I moved him to Madison County where I found him a place to live and a job. He was quite content but wanted his wife to move to Madison County.

They had a court hearing in Montgomery County to get custody of their kids. Jackie had given his attorney his address in Madison County. That was a fatal mistake. My investigation showed that another attorney in the same office as Jackie's attorney got the address and gave it to one of the brothers and his dad.

On December 18, 1993 one of the brothers and his father came to Madison County. They went to where Jackie Martin was living. The father went to the front door of Jackie's house while Jackie was wrapping Christmas presents for his children. He shot through the front door killing Jackie Martin.

I was working my part time job when I got the radio traffic. I was told to call station and was asked if I had an informant that lived on south county road 300 East. I said I did.

I was told Jackie had been murdered. I could not believe it. I went to Jackie's home and when I saw him I had mixed emotions. I was angry that the crime family had done this. I was hurt for his family. I blamed myself and felt like I had let Jackie down.

I prayed to God and asked for peace, wisdom, and the strength to find who had done this. I requested scene techs to work the crime scene. Randy Simmons and I proceeded to Crawfordsville.

We could not find who I thought had done it but we started building the case. For the next three weeks I worked in Crawfordsville to assemble the case against the father and son who had killed Jackie.

Randy Simmons and I learned the son and his friend, whose prints had been lifted from the stolen truck, were up by East Chicago picking up a vehicle. We proceeded there and spoke with both men. The son and I got into a heated discussion. He said he did not commit the murder but someone bigger than him did "Point Dot!" That was the way this suspect had of finishing his sentences with emphasis – "Point Dot" as if he were trying to stick the defiant words in my eye. I responded with, "So, it was your father who committed the murder – Point Dot!"

I knew there were threats being made against my life, but God gave me the strength to make that trip to Crawfordsville every day. There were days I was exhausted, but with Randy Simmons and Detective Bob Blount's help I made the trip. I stopped by a possible witness' house just about every day.

The attorney who later told us about getting Jackie's address and giving it to the father and son would show up and say I could not talk to anyone because he was representing them.

One day when I was talking with a witness the attorney showed up and said I could not talk to the witness. I called Prosecutor William F. Lawler. I asked him how long I had to put up with this attorney. Mr. Lawler said if I was not arresting the person or reading them their rights the attorney did not have to be there.

I started back into the room to talk with the witness. The attorney started to follow me. I told him he was not needed and when I was ready I was going to talk to him and he would need his own attorney.

One day, when Randy Simmons and I were meeting Sheriff Rice to discuss our next move, I received a phone call. It was about the man whose prints were on the stolen truck – the man I had visited about every day that I was in Crawfordsville. He had been arrested several days before in Clinton County on an old charge.

The woman calling me was the wife of the son who been involved in Jackie's murder. She said her husband and his attorney were in Clinton County trying to get the guy out of jail so they could kill him. They were afraid he would talk to me about the murder.

I called the prosecutor's office. I talked to deputy prosecutor Jim Nave and prosecutor William Lawler. We discussed the case and I was told to arrest the father and his son.

We went to Clinton County to the court house and the son was arrested. The attorney gave a statement which was helpful in the investigation. The father could not be found.

The son was later taken to trial. He was found guilty. He cooperated to avoid the death penalty. He gave up his father and told us where he could be located.

The father was arrested in Lake Ozark, Missouri. Warrants had been issued for Jackie Martin's murder. The father surrendered to police who telephoned the residence after calling in reinforcements to surround the area. This was under the authority of Captain Clarence Greeno of the Missouri State Police. Sergeant Bill Harp and I went and transported the father back to Madison County.

In April I charged three other people who had been involved in the alleged conspiracy.

The father of the man already convicted of murder was taken to trial. The jury found him guilty as well. He was facing the death penalty. Both men went to prison.

I remember thanking God when the apprehensions and trials were over. Despite the attorney trying to interfere with my investigation, and threats being made on my life, God gave me the opportunities and the strength to bring Jackie Martin's killers to justice.

Still the victory was tainted for me. Jackie Martin, this imperfect man, had put his life on the line to help us convict one of the most brutal crime families in Indiana. He was under my care when he was murdered. That's why this letter from his niece meant so much to me.

Misty Lester September 27, 2010. Hi Mr. Hanna, I am the niece of Jackie Martin. For years I have been searching for any info on my uncle's murder. Upon a Google search I found that you are at part, if not all responsible in bringing his killers to justice. For that, I want to say thank you from the bottom of my heart. Also, I was a teenager at the time and my mother would never speak of any details, etc. I am now 30 years old and I think of him very often and would like more details if you have a chance to ever speak with me to help me be at peace.

Thank you,

Misty

Most people would look at Jackie as a punk criminal. I'm glad that God doesn't see people that way. Who am I to tell God he made a mistake in creating that one? Jackie not only deserved my respect, he earned it.

* * * * * *

A person doesn't have to sacrifice their life to be heroic. Sometimes a kind word at the time it is needed can be one of the greatest gifts a person can give to "save" another human being.

In the late '70s and early '80s I was part of a panel discussion at the Law Enforcement Academy. I finished one of those sessions and headed back to Madison County. I still had several hours before my shift ended, so I started patrolling when I got back.

I was in the area of 9th and John streets, westbound, when I noticed the car in front of me. The car was so left of center I had to check to make sure it was still a two way street and hadn't been changed to a one way.

I put my emergency lights on to stop the car. It sped up and ran through the stop sign. When we reached Madison Avenue the car in front of me turned south then westbound in an alley. We were driving at a high rate of speed. I almost hit a telephone so I slowed down.

We were now in the alley several blocks west of Madison Avenue. The car in front of me flipped then rolled coming to a stop. I ran to the car and found three occupants.

The driver wasn't seriously injured. He was uninsured, which was the likely reason he took off like he did. The male in the passenger seat broke both of his legs and was in quite a bit of pain. The young lady who was in the middle of the front seat was unconscious.

25

Greater Love Has No One Than This

I attempted CPR on the young lady because she had stopped breathing. I tried to revive her but was unsuccessful. She died in my arms. I was crushed.

I blamed myself. I asked God why this had happened. The young girl dying tore me up inside. I went to Community Hospital to follow up on the accident victims. The young lady's sister came up to me and hugged me.

She told me not to blame myself. She said her sister picked who she ran with. She also said her sister had picked her lifestyle instead of taking care of her children.

I then went to the Madison County jail. I advised the driver of the Implied Consent Law. He was then offered a breathalyzer test. He took it and failed.

The driver then asked the condition of the passengers of his vehicle. I told him that the other male passenger (his brother) had broken both of his legs and the female had been killed. He started laughing.

I prayed to God for strength. I prayed for patience. I prayed for forgiveness. I prayed for compassion.

I cried that night. God showed me I was not responsible for the young lady's life but I hurt for her kids, sister, and her family. Through God's grace I even hurt for the driver of the vehicle.

The sister of the woman who died could have gone off on me. She could have ignored me altogether. Instead she gave me words of assurance. I knew I wasn't to blame. It was almost certain that that driver would have hurt someone that day. I could justify it a thousand ways, but it still hurt to know I couldn't save that young woman.

Those words of encouragement from her sister might have been a small sacrifice to her, but they meant the world to me.

Chapter 4

Who Hunger and Thirst for Justice

God blesses those who hunger and thirst for justice, for they will be satisfied. – Matthew 5:6 (NLT)

As you can see from my chapter on Jackie Martin, when I get a burr under my saddle for justice I don't rest until justice is served.

In the following passage I will refer to the suspect only as the suspect or in some generic terms to avoid embarrassing the family. This suspect has since died in prison and his family are truly good people. It seems heartless to me to cause them more pain, but the victim deserves to be remembered.

This particular suspect had been arrested for battery. He went to trial and was acquitted. He showed up on my door step to shovel the snow. He said that God gave him a second chance and he wanted to repay me for always being kind to him. He later was investigated by the Edgewood Police Department for stealing checks and money from friends of his parents. He would use the excuse that he needed the money for his child.

October 11, 1997, the suspect tied seventy-eight-year-old Maxine Heitger's arms and legs to her bed, stuffed tissue into her mouth and taped her mouth shut. The suspect then stole Heitger's credit card and automobile. Heitger died of asphyxiation. I was called out to investigate the case. On my way to the scene I knew, because of the location of the crime scene, that this man was my suspect.

After seeing Maxine Heitger I was furious to see how the killer had treated her. It could have been my mom or grandmother. I asked God for strength, patience, and to be professional. In cases like these it is human to think revenge, but an officer must always get his revenge through properly applied justice.

While investigating the murder I was told that two young African-Americans had been stopped in the stolen car in Delaware County. I then thought I was wrong about my original hunch being the suspect in this murder case. I started focusing on the two young men in the stolen car as my suspects.

I was given the names of the two men. When we found one of the men, he identified my suspect as the man who had given them the car. He also showed detectives Simmons, Blount, and I where the suspect could be located.

Detective Blount stayed with the man who had shown us the location. Detective Simmons took the back door and I went to the front door. The suspect saw me coming. He ran to the back and saw detective Simmons. He then charged me and tried to run over me. That was a bad decision. I pulled him outside and took him to the ground at gun point.

The suspect was charged with and convicted of murder, felony murder, two counts of theft, robbery, burglary, and criminal confinement. The jury recommended that the suspect receive life without parole. The trial court subsequently sentenced him to sixty-five years in prison.

I felt bad because I knew this man's family. That's the hard part of justice served. There are often good people from the family, parents, siblings, and the like, who also suffer with the conviction. Still I remember seeing Maxine Heitger and I thanked God for giving me the strength and wisdom to do my job. God is good.

* * * * * *

I remember another "Thirst for Justice" case that really hit close to home.

Roger Nodine was a jail officer with Madison County Sheriff's Department. He had been dating a female reserve officer from the Henry County Sheriff's department. There had been trouble in the relationship and Roger started dating around.

On November 5, 1984, Roger's new girlfriend went to see him at about 5:30 A.M. When his ex-girlfriend pulled into the driveway, she saw an unfamiliar car and decided to talk to Roger away from the trailer. She parked her car and went by Officer Nodine's trailer. She told him she had car trouble and asked his help. They sat in her car and talked about their relationship. She was very upset because, although she had agreed Roger could see others, she was shocked to see the other woman's car in his driveway. The Henry County reserve officer told police that at that point, "she lost it" and admitted to shooting Roger Nodine. Ballistics tests confirmed Nodine was shot with her service revolver.

A neighbor, Clifford Randolph, heard loud voices and drove down his long driveway to investigate. He saw Nodine lying on the ground in front of one car. Officer Nodine had been shot but was able to speak. His ex-girlfriend had her hand under her jacket as if she had been shot. She ran up to Randolph, and said that she had been shot, and asked him to call an ambulance. Randolph drove next door to use the telephone and within 30 seconds he heard another shot from the direction of the cars. Mr. Randolph called the police and gave a description of the female with Nodine. Officer Nodine was pronounced dead at the hospital. He received six gunshot wounds, any one of which could have been fatal.

I located the female that had been at the crime scene at her grandmother's house. The reserve officer gave me her service revolver and a .25 caliber pistol and agreed to go to the police station. Deputy Carl Sells observed the suspect's automobile parked outside and noticed a reddish substance that appeared to be blood on the right side, down the right fender, and along the entire passenger side. I read the reserve officer her Miranda Rights and asked her about the red marks. The possible suspect said she didn't know anything about them, but later, said the blood was from an animal she had hit a week or more earlier. I told her he had to tow the car to find out about the blood she said that would be fine. Later on, when I talked to her and mentioned towing her car, she said it was done with her permission.

Deputy Dale Stegner watched the car until it was towed. Before it was towed, State Trooper George Boaz lifted some of the reddish substance from the car because he was afraid it might be lost when transporting the car to the jail. No warrant had been obtained to search the car. The car was taken to the garage of the Henry County Jail. When a search warrant for the vehicle arrived that afternoon, a state trooper recovered another sample of the same substance. The substance taken from the automobile was human blood of a type consistent with the blood that had soaked Officer Nodine's shirt.

The reserve officer agreed to talk to me after being read her Miranda Rights waiver. She made admissions as to her involvement in the case. I arrested her and she was later convicted of the crime.

I attended the autopsy of my friend Roger Nodine. It was one of the saddest and hardest things I ever had to do as a law enforcement officer. I prayed to God for strength. It was another senseless human tragedy, but justice was served.

* * * * * *

You might think that a fellow in law enforcement would eventually get jaded by these crimes. We don't. There was one particularly heinous crime that got under my skin and put me on an all out search for swift and sure justice. This one HAD to be solved, and soon.

On the afternoon of February 25, 2004 I was following up on a burglary. I heard a call on my radio and proceeded to the duplex where Cory Clark and her 3-year-old daughter were alone in their home near Lapel. Her 7-year-old daughter was at school and her husband was outside the state. Someone had entered the residence and used a knife to slit the throat of Cory Clark, then chased down 3-year-old Jenna and slit her throat as well. It was evident someone had attempted to rape Cory before her death.

I walked through the residence and saw Cory and her daughter with their throats slit. I prayed to God, asking for wisdom and strength. I asked why did this happen? I was standing over the little girl and I promised her I would not sleep until I found who had done this.

As we talked with neighbors, we were told about a man asking for directions to a construction site. We learned the man had an orange construction jacket on with a construction hard hat. We were told he was driving a small car with a handicap sticker in the front window. Another lady came to the scene and described the same guy who had been to her house earlier in the day. She said he tried to work his way into her house by asking to use her phone, but her dog scared him away. She felt threatened by him.

The mayor of Elwood, Indiana was in the area and stopped by the crime scene. He told me of a man who was lost and fitting the description of our possible suspect. He said the man acted energized like he was on something. I went home and showered and got cleaned up. I then went back out early in the morning and found a small construction site where several men were gathering. I called them over and talked to them. I described who I was looking for and they said he had worked there the day before and left and came back four to five hours later. I was told his name was Fred Baer.

I then called the company Fred Baer was working for in Indianapolis. His boss said he had talked with Fred and had fired him for leaving the job site the day before. I asked if Fred still had any of the company's property. I was told yes. I was told Fred was going to bring it back later because he was at the hospital in Southern Indiana.

I then called Baer and talked with him myself. I told him I had to talk with him about an incident that had happened the day before. He said he could meet in a couple days. I contacted the Governor's fugitive task force.

Through technology they located where Fred Baer was. We went to the location. They asked if I wanted to go in to get him and I said they could because I had seen the young child with her throat cut. Fred Baer was apprehended by the fugitive task force and they carried him out to where I was located. I prayed to God and thanked him for answering my prayers.

I had Baer show me where his car was located. I had a wrecker tow it back to Madison County. A search warrant was executed on the car and two blood samples were located. One of the blood DNAs was consistent with Cory Clark's daughter's blood.

That was an eerie discovery. When I saw the girl's body in her home I had made her a solemn promise that I would catch the man who had killed her and her mom. I felt like that blood sample was the little girl's finger pointing to Baer and telling me, "That's the man."

Detective Dave Callahan executed a search warrant on the apartment where Fred Baer lived. He found a trophy bag belonging to Fred Baer. It contained evidence of several rapes in Marion and Hamilton counties.

My investigation showed Baer had been working at a nearby construction site that day, left work, committed the murders, and then returned to the job. The apparent motive was to feed a drug habit and a deviant sexual appetite.

A man working another construction site I had contacted had seen Cory Clark bring trash out to the street. He saw the car driven by Baer stop suddenly. He then saw the car pull into a driveway near Cory Clark's residence.

Fred Baer was later tried and found guilty. At his sentencing hearing he was given the death penalty.

It was amazing that we had caught Fred Bair so quickly. I'm glad we did, for I would have looked until the day I died. I had made a heartbroken promise to a 3-year-old girl. The only solace I could give her was justice.

Chapter 5

With God All Things Are Possible

Jesus looked at them and said, "With man this is impossible, but with God all things are possible." – Matthew 19:26 (NIV)

"48-16"
(*My identifying number*)

"I'VE BEEN SHOT"

"CODE FIVE"

I was losing blood and I was floating into a state of shock. This was going to be the worst day of my life, or the last day of my life, or the most grace filled day of my life. The dispatcher's voice was my thin connection to mortal life. I will forever be grateful for that voice on the other end of the radio.

It was November 19, 1978, a crazy day in the cosmos. It was the same day as the Jonestown disaster, where the charismatic minister Jim Jones ordered the execution of a U.S. Congressman and for all of his flock to commit suicide. Only two days before, two Burger Chef employees were executed in their Indianapolis store – a crime that is still unsolved.

My wife Lori and I had been married one day short of six months. We were preparing to go to church on that cold Sunday morning. I had been a police officer just shy of four years on the Madison County Sheriff's department.

I received a phone call from the Madison County Sheriff's department dispatcher. I was told there had been a jail break and that three men had broken out of jail. The dispatcher then told me the jail officer on duty had been hurt during the escape.

I went to station where I picked up pictures of the escaped prisoners and background history on each one. I then picked up reserve officer Chuck McKissick who was a fireman on the Anderson City Fire Department. He rode with me the rest of the day.

With God All Things Are Possible

I had been called out around 9 a.m. on Sunday morning. I worked 4 p.m. to midnight as my assigned shift but had been called in early because of the three men who had escaped from custody.

The Sheriff's department was a small department at this time and the shift would consist of a dispatcher, jail officer, a supervisor, and two to four patrol officers to cover an area of 450 square miles.

On this particular day, on second shift, we were going to have a jail officer and two patrolmen working so one patrolman was going to have to dispatch the calls. David Kane, who had worked for the Madison County Sheriff's Department at one time, was a dispatcher for the Indiana State Police. I was going to be in charge of the second shift because I was the senior patrolman, so to keep two patrolman on the road I offered David Kane, who had the day off, a steak dinner if he would run radio for second shift. He agreed.

The first shift officers looked for the escapees all day. By 4 p.m. they had not been located so most of the officers had gone home. That left me with Chuck McKissick, Patrolman Randy Simmons, and Sergeant Harp riding in another car to continue looking for the escapees. We followed up on leads and contacted friends and relatives of the escaped inmates.

We had talked with a young lady earlier in the day who was a friend of one of the escaped men. Around 6 p.m. she called the Madison County dispatcher. She gave a location of where the three escaped inmates were held up in Alexandria, a small town approximately 11 miles north of Anderson, where the inmates had been housed at the Madison County jail.

We formed a team to approach the residence in Alexandria. The team included Chuck McKissick and I, Sergeant Harp, Patrolman Simmons, Patrolman Dennis Maxey and his wife Doris who also worked in the Madison County jail, and Patrolman Tim Davis with Officer Chris Malley.

We had been told the inmates might be armed. During the day it was getting progressively colder, and the escapees were hiding in an abandoned house without heat. They were not armed and they knew they were surrounded. I think it was for all these reasons that they surrendered without incident.

After the men had been returned to the Madison County jail, several of us decided to go to Frisch's Big Boy for supper. This was around 8 p.m. in the evening. We finished the meal and I had a little over two hours left in my shift. I took Chuck McKissick home and was going to finish my shift as quietly as possible. It had been a long and stressful day for the Madison County Sheriff's Department. The worst was behind us. What could go wrong in just two hours on a cold night? I would shortly receive the answer to that question.

* * * * * *

I was given a call on south Main Street in Anderson of a suspicious vehicle. When I arrived in the area the car was gone so I went to the complainant's house. He gave a pretty detailed description of the vehicle in question. He had also said it looked as though the occupants in the vehicle had been arguing – so much for a quiet finish to the shift.

I drove around the area and was initially unable to locate the vehicle in question. As I was about to quit looking for the vehicle I located it on Main Street In the area of I-69. I pulled in behind it, put on my red lights, and and hit the siren several times. The vehicle I was behind pulled into a driveway just north of I-69 on Main Street on the west side of the road.

The driver was Joe Thompson. His passenger was Marion Booth. As I was talking to Joe a man came out of the house. I knew him well. His name was Jerry Phagen. He was known to the area law enforcement. He called himself a held over hippy and was a small time drug dealer.

I told Jerry to go back into the residence. I also told him that he had nothing to do with the traffic stop and that he needed to mind his own business. Joe Thompson told Jerry to call his uncle who was a state trooper because he was going to jail.

Because it was so cold out I had Joe Thompson come back to sit in my police car while I checked his driver's license. I thought he might be driving on a suspended license, or that he had been drinking. I wanted him in my car to see if I could smell alcohol about his person.

I asked Joe for his driver's license and at first he remained quiet. I started to call dispatch to see if he was suspended or wanted for anything when he said he had a license. He reached in his back right pocket and pulled out a .25 caliber semi automatic pistol. He pointed his gun at me and ordered me to give him my gun. Then he yelled at me to give him "my damn gun." I told him to "Go to hell." It was certainly possible that he could have killed me with his .25, but it would have been a done deal if he had shot me with my .357 magnum service revolver. I was now in a fight for my life.

Because I had been called out earlier in the day while getting ready for church I was wearing a white shirt and black pants. I also had on my uniform jacket. Prior to eating supper I had a shoulder holster on, but had taken it off when I went into the restaurant to eat. I had stuck my gun in my belt when I had approached the car during the traffic stop.

Joe Thompson shot me six times while sitting next to me in my police car at point blank range.

The first bullet hit me on the left side of my face not a half an inch below my eye.

The second bullet hit my face on the left side of my chin.

My only chance to live was to get Joe's gun or to make him leave the car.

I started hitting Joe and was grabbing for the gun. He shot again. This time I was then hit in my right forearm and my right wrist. The bullets went right through my arm. The spent projectiles were later found in my coat and the police car.

I was then hit in my left forearm and again the bullet went through my arm.

With God All Things Are Possible

The last bullet went into my left shoulder and is still somewhere in my body.

My right arm went numb. This was significant because I shoot right handed. As Thompson ran away from my car I exited my car and pulled my gun out of my waistband. I shot at Joe four times. I missed him as he ran off into the night. I saw the woman that Joe Thompson had been arguing with, Marion Booth, exit the car and run towards I-69.

I had counted my shots as we were taught at the academy so I knew I had two rounds left in my revolver. I felt secure but also vulnerable. I sat back in my car and radioed I had been shot Code 5. Code 5 means either officer needs help, or officer down. I gave a description of the man who had shot me. Then I heard someone walk up on me. It was Jerry Phagen. He asked if I wanted a blanket and he covered me up even though I had my gun pointed at him. At that point I didn't know who to trust, but I now appreciate his kind gesture. I'm sure it also helped me medically as it was cold outside and I was going into shock.

It seemed like forever before any help arrived but David Kane, who was running the radio, kept talking to me. I felt even better when I heard my Captain, Dick Whetsel, come on the air stating he was en route to my location. Two Anderson city police officers arrived and stayed with me until the ambulance arrived. When the ambulance arrived the firemen and city police officers tried to lift me out of my car but I finally got out on my own and walked to the cot next to the ambulance.

I have gone to church all my life. I actually gave my life to Christ when I attended Anderson College (Now known as Anderson University) one Sunday morning at the Eastside Church of God. As I sat in my police car looking at my blood soaked white shirt I remember saying to God that I loved him and to let his will be done. I worried about my right arm being numb, felt a bullet hole right under my left eye, and did not think I was going to live.

I felt myself going into shock, but did not lose consciousness. I told the ambulance attendants that my doctor was Dr. Robert

McCurdy, a local surgeon. He had been our football team doctor at Anderson College. I asked the ambulance crew to take me to Community Hospital where I had worked as a part time security officer. I knew God was in control but he allowed me to have a say as to what was going to happen.

We arrived at Community Hospital. As they were rolling me in the door I felt something drop into my mouth. I thought was a tooth but as I pulled Patrolman Tim Davis' hand over to my mouth I spit out a .25 caliber projectile into his hand. I remember saying to God under my breath thank you and to let his will be done.

Officer Doris Maxey had ridden in the ambulance with me to the hospital. I was worried about how my wife would be told because she would just be getting home from work. I was afraid she might have even heard it on the radio on her way home. Her father had been a quadriplegic all of her life and we had only been married six months. This was going through my head so I asked Doris to please go tell her so someone would not just call her.

My mother and father had been in North Carolina and had just gotten home when they had been told about the shooting. My father was a retired Anderson police officer. I was concerned my father might blame himself because of what happened.

The shooting happened on Sunday night. The following Thursday was Thanksgiving. Dr. McCurdy came into my hospital room Thanksgiving morning and asked if I wanted turkey for lunch. I said I did, thinking it would be hospital turkey. He said I thought you would and discharged me from the hospital.

I had six bullet wounds with three exit wounds. I was out of the hospital in three days. Not one surgery. The worst thing I had to endure were the soaks that had to be put on all the wounds several times a day. It was worse for my wife and the nursing staff than it was for me.

I had usually had Thanksgiving dinner at my parent's house. Because of just getting home from the hospital, Lori said she would make it for me. She had to go shopping and cook it in one day and it was awesome – the best Thanksgiving of my life.

With God All Things Are Possible

Sometimes it is hard to think of all of the things you are thankful for. That day it was easy.

As I thought about being shot six times, one bullet missing my left eye by an inch, spitting a bullet out at the hospital, not going into shock, no surgeries, going home in three days, and no infection with six entrance and three exit wounds. I kept saying this verse to myself:

Jesus looked at them and said, "With man this is impossible, but with God all things are possible." – Matthew 19:26 (NIV)

On the night of the shooting Joe Thompson was found and arrested in a barn maybe 200 yards from where the shooting took place.

I went back to work several weeks after the shooting. The gun had not been located so Lt. Pete Dodd, Lt. Roger Noland, and I went back to the area of the shooting. We used a metal detector and methodically walked a corn field. We did not find the gun. As we were preparing to leave I went to a large tree to urinate and as I looked down I saw a .25 caliber semi automatic handgun. I collected it and ballistics later showed that it was the gun Joe Thompson had used to shoot me.

Joe Thompson was given a long sentence for his crime. For the rest of my life I will remember the details of that day and how close it came to being my last. Still there is another person who was deeply marked by that day. Several years after the shooting my wife, Lori wrote these words:

Before Sam's shooting I was very anxious every time Sam went out the door. I was acutely aware that every time I kissed him goodbye, it might be the last time. I had been taught faith, and lived with a family that lived by faith, but wasn't quite sure what that meant for me. I would anxiously listen to the scanner and breathe a sign of relief when he was home.

After Sam was shot, people arrived at the hospital that he hadn't seen since kindergarten – in part I believe just to see what someone who had been shot six times looked like! I had

39

worked ICU and had seen someone die of only one gunshot. That had been an infected gunshot, so with six gunshots I wasn't terribly hopeful. Sam not only survived but also did not get even one infection. He was too shocky to even get an IV in.

Looking at someone who has been shot six times and survived, you realize you are looking at a miracle. There was no amount of worry that produced his protection. God was his protection. God willed Sam to live. It was as if God was telling me, "Trust me, I've got this." From that time forward I trusted God's continual protection.

Sam has always said he works from his "gut." It didn't take me long to realize that "gut" feeling was God leading Sam.

Many of us are not as in tune to hearing this voice. This voice, I have believed, is the Holy Spirit giving direction and guidance and I am grateful to be married to a Godly man who is in tune with, and listening to, God's direction.

Our family has learned that when Sam has been called away by the many cases he has worked it was a sacrifice that we made to help Sam help our community, the people in it, and to ultimately make our community safer.

* * * * * *

Needless to say, I chose a good wife.

Chapter 6

Sowing Seeds

"A farmer went out to sow his seed. As he was scattering the seed, some fell along the path; it was trampled on, and the birds ate it up. Some fell on rocky ground, and when it came up, the plants withered because they had no moisture. Other seed fell among thorns, which grew up with it and choked the plants. Still other seed fell on good soil. It came up and yielded a crop, a hundred times more than was sown." – Luke 8:5-8 (NIV)

Madison County is an even mixture of large and small towns surrounded by good farmland. Harvesting corn and herding cattle is not an uncommon sight out in the county. I just never imagined I'd ever do both with a patrol car. Anyone who lived near 200 East and 500 North in 1976 will remember that swath that was cut out of the cornfield that September. Here is that story.

Madison County Police Department Deputy Robert Sapp received a call that someone was passed out in a car near 600 North and Indiana 9. Deputy Sapp was driving a 1974 GMC van that had been purchased by the county Explorer Scouts. It had been equipped with red lights, siren, radio, and emergency equipment.

When Deputy Sapp located the reported vehicle he found the driver inside and apparently drunk. He advised the driver that he was under arrest for intoxication. The man became rowdy, assaulted the deputy, and stole the county van. He then proceeded south on Indiana 9.

I was called in to give chase. To add insult to injury, there was a nationwide gas shortage and we were limited on how much fuel we could buy at a time. I took the call, but I had to stop at a gas station and squeeze in a quick $5.00 worth of gasoline before I could join the chase. When I got within range I was sideswiped by the van and was pushed across the highway divider.

It was clear that this guy wasn't going to give up easily. The drunk driver turned the van around and started traveling south on

41

Indiana 9 again. Then he headed back onto the county roads. We chased him for more than 30 minutes at speeds of up to 100 m.p.h. It was clear that this wasn't going to end well. I knew for a fact that it wasn't going to end well for the fleeing suspect.

In an attempt to further elude police, the driver drove the van off County Road 200 East. He drove 1,650 feet through a cornfield where he slammed through a fence, skidded across the road and crashed into a deep ditch on the east side of the road, 350 feet north of County Road 500 North. Six Madison County police cars and several city units responded to the call before he was taken back into custody. County officer Mike McKain and I were also assaulted by the man when all of us pursuing police attempted to arrest him.

A herd of cattle owned by Charles Lawler were being taken down County Road 200 East to another grazing spot when the driver slammed through the fence at that high rate of speed. The herd was about 100 feet away, and could have been slaughtered had he not wrecked the vehicle. The cattle were taken back to their original grazing land until the roadway could be cleared.

It was a miracle that nobody had been hurt, and that those cattle had been saved. The farmer lost several bushels of his corn, but it could have been much worse. Even the suspect refused treatment when he was taken to the hospital

The driver was arrested on charges of auto banditry, and driving while under the influence. Around 15 other moving traffic violations were tacked on before it was over. He had obviously sown some bad seed that day in that cornfield.

* * * * * *

This would be a good time to tell you more about my colleague and friend Mike McKain. Mike looked like Steve McQueen and had a lively sense of humor. He was the kind of fellow who stands out in life and makes you think, "Wow, what a great guy!"

When you start a job like I did with the Madison County Sheriff's Department there is someone who will take time to help train you. The first patrolman who allowed me to ride with him as a reserve, and then a jail officer, was Patrolman Mike McKain. I rode with him every Friday evening.

He taught me how to clean a police car and shine up a uniform for inspection. I was also taught by Mike what was important and what was not. For instance one night we stopped a farm tractor pulling a disc. I asked if we were going to write the driver a ticket and he told me that farmers have a tough job and we do not want to make it worse. He said we should give him a verbal warning and ask them to slow down, have the proper signage for slow moving vehicles, or stay on his side of the road.

Even though I was only a jail officer at the time, Mike taught me how to lift fingerprints. I was also shown how to write a ticket. When we went to a crime scene he gave me his camera, showed me how to use it, and told me to take pictures of everything then take them again to make sure I had not missed anything.

One night I was patrolling with Mike and he was not feeling well. We met with his captain and got permission so I could drive Mike around the rest of the shift. Minutes later we tried to stop an intoxicated driver and ended up in a pursuit. After we stopped the vehicle Mike told me the arrest was mine because I had earned it.

Mike and I became good friends. I admired him because he was a great family man. He adored his wife, Chris, and talked about her often.

He would say and do funny things that kept me laughing. Mike said numerous times that when there was a situation that needed that special officer "you call CODE 35," meaning Mike McKain.

There was another time we were sent on a call involving a stranded vehicle in the middle of the road. When we found the stranded vehicle it was surrounded and stuck in ice. Mike looked at me and said it was our job to go where no police officer has been before. As Mike started driving his car fell through the ice and black smoke rolled out from under the police car.

Mike took the time and taught me that police work is fun. He taught me how dangerous the job could be. He taught me to treat the people we arrested as human beings and would joke around with them.

I remember a couple of guys we arrested. Mike lectured them all the way to jail. As we put them in the cage in the booking area to wait to be processed, one of the young men said to Mike, "Who do you think you are, SUPERMAN?" Mike turned towards the young man, unzipped his uniform shirt, and showed the young man the Superman t-shirt he was wearing.

I believe God puts people in your life to help you reach the goal he has set forth for your life. I miss Mike. He, his wife, and daughter were in an accident after dropping his son off at Purdue. Mike was killed. I had been to a family reunion in Pennsylvania. We came back on Sunday and I went to work Monday. When I got to work I could tell something was wrong. Everyone was quiet and when I asked why I learned of Mike's death.

I can still feel that moment. That's why I am dedicating this book to Mike McKain. Mike was my friend and my teacher. I think of him often. He took an interest in me and invested his time with me to make me a better police officer and a better man. Thank You, Mike McKain.

* * * * * *

The best sowing a man can do is to follow Mike's advice to treat people, even the ones we arrest, as human beings. There are many victims in a crime or at an accident scene. There are the victims themselves, and certainly their family and friends. It's easy to forget that the perpetrator has a family – many times good people who are hurt by what their loved ones have done. While some criminals are just plain evil, many are basically good people who have made a mistake or a series of bad choices. An officer who makes good choices and takes a human interest in each situation can make a real difference to offset those bad choices. I would like to share with you some of the notes I have received over the years that show the value of good sowing. I don't do this to brag, but to show young officers what a difference they can make in their service if they never forget the human side of our business.

Sowing Seeds

From Stephanie Howells:

I was between 3 and 4 years old, my mother was married to an abusive man, she NEVER thought he would harm me. But one day my grandma and aunt picked me up, so my mom could go to work, and noticed obvious bruises all over my little body, so they took me to the emergency room. It was investigated and found that I had been abused by my mom's husband.

Mr. Sam Hanna was the investigating officer, and promised my family this man would be held accountable for what he had done to me and my mother. I was placed in my grandmother's custody, and this prompted my mother, to do what she should have done earlier, to leave this man. You see this man had my mother so scared, that she thought he would cause harm to other members of our family. But Sam reassured her that if she took all necessary steps to ensure he paid for harming me, that he in return would guarantee all of our safety, and mom said he kept that very promise. That man made threats and attempted to follow through on some of them, but none of us were ever harmed by him ever again.

My mother was able to divorce him, and go through counseling to notice early signs of abuse. My mother gained custody of me back after awhile. I graduated with honors, went to college, got married, and had 3 beautiful healthy children. I now work with special needs children, all possible because of Sam Hanna going above and beyond the call of duty.

Thank you seems so trivial, but thank you to this man, he has never been forgotten over these years. I myself don't remember the events of being abused, thank goodness. I'm not sure if it was because I was so young, or my mind just blocked it out, but regardless Sam Hanna has been and will always be one of my personal heroes!!!

From Debra Stafford Ellis:

I remember you as a young man just starting with the Madison County Sheriff's Department. You came in nearly every night you worked. I worked at the Village Pantry in Alexandria. You were always very nice – never arrogant and very respectful. The best part was when my friend and I teased you when you told us you were getting married. There are probably more people than you realize that have met you someway and have paid attention to your career and are proud to know you once crossed their path. You also arrested my son and never judged me. You were one that told me if I don't let go I was going to love him to death and to detach with that love and live knowing we are all responsible for our own actions and the consequences of them. You also mentored my nephew that started his job as a detective today. God bless you man.

From Joe Fisher:

My parents were amazing parents that taught me right from wrong, (and spanked me when needed). They were there when I was in pain, had a kind word when I was down, and made sure I knew the awesomeness that is Jesus, and to this day they are still there for me no matter what, just as I am there for my family.

Despite all that as we all know, when I was 18 I was an idiot and did stupid things and got arrested. My arresting officer was Samuel Hanna. It bugs me that I've heard some people talking trash about him even though I know that comes with his job. When Sam arrested me he could have taken me straight to jail but he didn't, he took me to my parents' house and made me explain to them what I did so I could see the pain and disappointment it caused, he then drove the long route to jail to talk to me about honesty and integrity and what it means to be a man – something he also didn't have to do. Then he talked to me about Christ and reminded me that he loved me despite my mistakes. He showed a level of compassion that day that just can't be faked. He wanted to be sure that this dumb kid, that was trying to act tough, never got into trouble again.

Since then I've worked hard to prove I am a good man, in doing so I've been blessed with a career in EMS in which I've gotten to work side by side with Sam who shows just as much compassion and care for everyone else as he did me. Even when he's being spit on and put down, he shows exactly what it means to have compassion and integrity. It is an honor to have been able to show him he was right about me, and to be able to work by his side on a few scenes. I am thankful that God led him into this career and that we are lucky to have him serving us in Madison county.

From Lora Kidwell:

A very long time ago Mr. Hanna pulled me over for the car I was driving being loud. It came back that I had a suspended license. I had taken care of that months before and was scared to death. I told him I had taken care of it and I had the money order copies at home. He took my word for it and gave me a ticket for not wearing my seatbelt. He told me to call and straighten it all out and I did the very next day. It meant a lot to me that he had faith that I was telling him the truth. He could have towed the car and taken me to jail. I'm so thankful he put faith in that I was telling him the truth.

From Cathy Baker:

My 4-year-old daughter wasn't at her grandparents' home where I was to pick her up after a weekend visit with her father. He had not seen her in 8 months, when he returned from his home state of Florida. He had visitation while in Madison County. My attorney introduced me to child advocate, Bennie Magers. Bennie encouraged me to keep pushing forward.

My life as I had known it was forever changed. Bennie had many contacts from years of tracking down missing children. I had no idea at the time what a favor my attorney had done for me.

Weeks turned into months, and I was desperate for someone, anyone, to listen to me. I had picked my brain and spent endless hours doing my own investigation. I asked my attorney to get any bank statements belonging to my ex. He did.

I spent day and night picking through those cancelled checks. I finally found a check written to a friend. I thought it was strange, considering my ex-husband never let go of a dime.

I told Bennie I felt there was something up with the check paid to my ex-husband's friend. We made a trip to the Board of Health and found that John S had gotten a duplicate birth certificate 3 months before Elizabeth was taken.

I took the check and birth certificate information to one agency and was told to let them do their job. I could not get anyone to listen! I knew this man better than anyone! Bennie knew I was hanging by a thread. It was agony trying to lie down to sleep not knowing where my precious child was or if I would ever see her again! I was just flat out exhausted, and Bennie knew it.

I gathered all my scratch pads and 15 lb briefcase and walked out of the agency. Bennie had had enough too. She said, "Come on, we're going to see Sam Hanna!" She was fed up with no one listening and so was I.

Within minutes of walking into the Sheriff's department I was standing face to face with Sam. Sam listened as Bennie explained what we had found and what our theory was. By this time I was in tears. I thought, "What if Sam won't listen?"

Sam did listen! Within a matter of minutes Sam told us that we were in fact right about whose identity my ex had taken. From that day on I had hope. Sam investigated lead after lead and got the FBI involved in my case. This was a man passionate about serving without being the center of attention. From that day on I spoke with Sam daily. I can't tell you how many times Sam stopped whatever he was doing to encourage me and tell me "Yes, Cathy we will find her." I just needed to hear Sam say those words.

October 6, 1990 I got the news I had been praying for. My daughter had been found. She was in Globe, Arizona. A police officer saw a motor home parked behind a chamber of commerce in the early hours of the morning. She thought it looked suspicious, so she ran the plate. Sam's work had paid off! My daughter was asleep in the motor home. Her father had bleached her hair, changed her name, and was told that her family had been killed in a car accident.

I have my daughter and two beautiful grandchildren today because Sam listened and took on a job that he really didn't have to get involved in. That's just the kind of man Sam is. I'm honored and so thankful that our paths crossed. We need more Sam Hanna's in the world.

From Sondra Horn:

My name is Sondra Horn. I was born in 1962. My mother and father divorced when I was very young when I was 10-years-old my mother remarried.

At first he seemed like a good father. He taught me how to ride a horse and work hard. Things changed when I turned 14.

That is when he made me to start having sex with him. He told me he would kill my mother if I told anyone. I kept it to myself until I was about 20 years old. He continued to force me to have sex after I was 18-years-old.

I was working as a nurse's aide at a nursing home in Alexandria when he started messing with my younger sister. I knew then I could not let this happen.

I made friends with a co-worker by the name of Joy Sultz. When I felt comfortable with her, and thought I could trust her, I opened up to her. I told her what I was going through.

She put me in her car and took me directly to the Sheriff's Department to talk to Detective Sam Hanna. She had been told we could trust Sam Hanna and that he would do something about it.

Well, sure enough, he took my statement and worked the case. He arrested my stepdad. He was put in jail and when we went to court Sam was there for me. My stepdad got charged with 4 class A felonies. He got 30 years for each count.

Sam was there when no one else was. He has always been there when I needed him. When I got married he came to the wedding and he helped my husband and I to adopt our son.

He has always been like a big brother to me. He would check on me periodically to make sure I was okay. Sam is a good man who believes in God.

With Sam's help I have made it through the years remembering what he told me. Sam said to me "Never Give Up because if I do then I am letting them win." He would also say stay strong and that's what keeps me going even in rough times. Thank you Sam Hanna.

Again I am not sharing these to brag, but to show people, especially, law enforcement officers, the difference it makes when you treat people like human beings and put yourself in their place. I in turn had learned these lessons from Mike McKain and from Sheriff John Gunter who advised me to treat victims of tragedies as if you are talking to your own family.

I will end this chapter with one of those results that we all want to hear about but never seem to see on the news.

* * * * * *

Approximately two years prior to May 20, 1999 I became aware of a local motorcycle gang. The gang had been involved in burglaries, thefts, auto thefts and several drive-by shootings. The gang was responsible for over 50 burglaries in 6 counties.

The ATF, and one of the Madison County officers, had arrested one of the older gang members several months before I had started my investigation. The gang had not slowed down. They were still stealing Harleys and breaking into houses with attached garages and new houses under construction.

After I took the report of another Harley Davidson theft I received further information that the cousin of Kevin Hummel was involved. I gathered enough evidence to arrest him. I started building my case using him as my informant. Daryl McCormick from the Anderson police department worked with me. We pulled cases from the county and city that were similar and looked at the similarities.

We worked closely with Chief Deputy Prosecutor Bryan Williams. Our evidence was pretty thin at that point, but Bryan trusted the investigation skills that Daryl and I had shown him in the past. He really went out on a limb for us and gave us the green light to bring in the gang members for questioning so we could bolster our case. Our main target was Kevin Hummel who was president of the motorcycle club. This investigation went on for over a year.

Sowing Seeds

We took statement after statement where the gang members implicated themselves and each other. I was building a pretty good circumstantial case on approximately ten gang members and associates. I even charged one man who was the fence for a lot of the stolen property.

One day Daryl and I pulled up in front of Kevin's house. We did not have to go up to the door. He had cameras all around his house. He saw me pull up and came outside.

He said to me that he had heard I wanted to see inside of his garage. I said no, I wanted him. I then told him that, when I got ready, I was going to arrest him and to have his bags packed as he was going to prison for a long time.

Daryl and I left. I wanted Kevin to know we were investigating him and that he was our main suspect. I also knew he had a city policeman leaking information to him and I was not sure who it was. I wanted him to know it didn't matter.

We finally got to the point to make our arrests. We took the paperwork to Bryan Williams and he filed the charges. A magistrate heard our probable cause then issued warrants.

We ended up filing charges on the group anywhere from one count of theft or burglary to approximately thirty counts on Kevin Hummel. We had Kevin on grinding off a tattoo on one gang member, and breaking the hands of another man who was supposed to buy drugs for him, but spent the money and bought no drugs. Kevin broke his hands with the man's own hammer. Kevin, and several other gang members, went to shoot at another gang's club house, and shot up a man's house that had nothing to do with any gang. It was only by the grace of God that the owner was at work instead of home and he was not hurt.

When Daryl and I went to arrest Kevin I decided to get Kevin away from his house because we had been told he had weapons. We pulled up in front of Kevin's house and Kevin came out holding one of his kids. I started walking towards Kevin's garage he started to follow me so I drew down on him. He kept asking us to not let his kids see what was happening.

Sowing Seeds

We ended up filing approximately thirty counts against Kevin Hummel – one of which was for Corrupt Business Practices. He ended up pleading guilty to all charges along with his codefendants except one who went to trial and was found guilty. Kevin was sentenced to over forty years in prison. The other defendants received either prison time or probation.

As they plead guilty the Judge ordered a cleanup statement. Kevin gave me his. As I started to take him back to jail Kevin asked me a favor. I thought he was crazy asking me for anything after I had spent over a year on this case, but I asked him what he wanted. He asked about what he could do to get out early. I was shocked and asked why. He said he had two boys and he wanted to get out to raise them so they would not turn out like he did. I was touched.

God showed me something I never expected. I told Kevin to go to prison and get his GED. Do anything to better himself and I would see what, if anything, I could do to get him out.

Every month or two I got a letter from Kevin. He let me know of his progress. I even got letters from his counselor.

Kevin was in prison for approximately ten years. I helped to get him out and he went to work in a local restaurant busing tables. This is a man who at one time had all the money or drugs he wanted. He was out of prison, working, and trying to raise his two sons.

Kevin and I started a group. It is called Second Chance to Get it Right. We raised money to fix up two parks and we do motorcycle rides every year to buy Christmas for a family and children who could not afford one. We raise money for school supplies to help kids go back to school each year. We sponsor a family each year for Thanksgiving.

Kevin loves going around talking to church groups, schools, and juvenile detention facilities. He wants to help children to make better choices than he made as a boy growing up. Kevin is giving back to the community he once victimized.

Sowing Seeds

Once again I learned to put my natural feelings toward a hardened criminal aside and to let God control the situation. God is loving and compassionate. That's a pretty good example to follow.

* * * * * *

An officer can make a big difference in the world if he knows when to be kind, when to be tenacious, and when to give a person a break. It's all a matter of sowing good seed.

Sowing Seeds

Chapter 7

It's a Job

In Christ Jesus, then, I have reason to be proud of my work for God. – Romans 15:17 (ESV)

Be strong and courageous. Do not be afraid or terrified because of them, for the LORD your God goes with you; he will never leave you nor forsake you.– Deuteronomy 31:6 (NIV)

If any of you lacks wisdom, let him ask God, who gives generously to all without reproach, and it will be given him. – James 1:5 (ESV)

I've used three verses here to define the work I've done in law enforcement. An officer must do his work with pride. You can't just be the big guy who hauls in the bad guys. An officer must be the person who pays attention to doing the job right so the system works for justice for all – even the perpetrator. Having pride in your work requires patience, preparation, and attention to detail.

A good officer must also be strong in the face of fear while being able to use the respect of fear to avoid making a bad situation worse. That one is harder to explain, but I will attempt to make it clearer with the examples in this chapter.

Finally, there are times when all of the human reason in the world cannot explain the heartbreaking situations that an officer must witness. I was torn apart and sick with grief when I saw that murdered three-year-old and her mother near Lapel. In that situation I was able to fight back by tracking down their killer. Sometimes, though, there just isn't anything an officer can do to balance the scene. In those times you just have to trust in a greater wisdom than the understanding of man.

You will see examples of all three of these scriptures in this chapter.

Police work is a job. Like any other job you have good days and bad days. Sometimes you take chances and they pay off. Sometimes you stumble. Sometimes it's God's grace that gets you through the shift. I took a real chance with this one.

It's a Job

I worked Wednesday evenings. This particular Wednesday my parents were out of town. I was going to check their house before I went home. As I sat at the stop light at 8th Street and John Street I saw a man run out of the liquor store. He ran to a car at the phone booth then back into the store.

I pulled in and talked to the people at the phone booth. They said the liquor store had just been robbed. As we looked towards the building, a man rode his bike from the back of the liquor store. The occupants of the car said the young man on the bike was the one who had robbed the liquor store.

I followed the bicycle and wondered what I would do if he stopped for me. My gun was in the trunk of my vehicle and earlier in the day I had a lump removed from a testicle and had staples where the lump had been removed.

The bike went up on the sidewalk behind several cars then back on the street. I confirmed by radio that there had been a robbery and this was the suspect. I put my red light on, hoping the suspect would not run. He stopped and walked back to my car. I grabbed him, disarmed him, and held him against my car until backup arrived. The man was arrested by the Anderson city police. The suspect had me at every turn. He could have easily shot me or overpowered me, but it turned out in my favor that day. I should have been afraid of the suspect. Instead I put on a face of strength and courage and made him fear me for an easy arrest. There isn't much of a gap between being a hero or a fool. That time I was able to use fear to my advantage.

* * * * * *

One sunny afternoon I was northbound on Broadway, with lights and siren on, going to an accident. I had been dispatched to a personal injury accident located at state road 9 and county road 500 north. As I approached Cross Street and State Road 9 another driver turned eastbound into my path of travel.

I turned away from the vehicle, hitting a telephone pole, bus bench, and phone booth. The other car then hit my police cruiser. I had my seat belt on but I hit my side window with my head.

It's a Job

I suffered a concussion and went to the hospital by ambulance. I was treated and released, and went back to work a week later. God gave me the strength to survive the accident and to return to work quickly.

I thought of another favorite Bible verse, *I can do all things through him who strengthens me.* – Philippians 4:13 (ESV)

There are two points I would like to make with this story. First, keep your body healthy and strong. It is God who gave me a strong body, but it is Sam who has to workout and keep that body fit. In doing so I have been able to survive these hits and heal faster.

The second point is a request to the general public. Police officers have had a lot of negative feelings tossed their way in recent years. It means a lot to us when people thank us and ask about how they can make our jobs easier. One of the best ways to help would be to keep aware of their surroundings when they are driving. I've been the investigator of too many accidents that were caused by a moment of inattention. Most of those, thank God, were fender benders. Some of them have been tragic and heartbreaking. So please yield to emergency vehicles in transit, and just as importantly, to each other.

* * * * * *

On another Wednesday evening while working I went to the county jail to get gas. As I approached the Eisenhower Bridge I noticed a car stopped in the road with the flashers on. The driver, a young African-American man, was out of the car and standing by the rail threatening to jump off the bridge. He also had a knife in his hand. He had had an argument with his girlfriend and was pretty distraught. All I had to do was to convince a man, out of his mind with grief, to give up the idea of jumping without also stabbing himself or me. Think about that the next time you are having a bad day at work.

I started to talk to him. The Anderson city police arrived. I was going to back off and let them deal with the situation since it was in the city.

57

It's a Job

The supervisor told me to continue what I was doing. I kept talking and, more importantly, listening to the young man as I inched my way towards him. I finally convinced him to give me the knife. Step one – that was a relief. Now I had to keep him from jumping and maybe taking me with him.

As I inched closer he backed away. It was getting down to the critical moment. If I moved too quickly, or was too far away, all would be lost. He finally backed into one of the light poles on the bridge railing and I had my chance. I lunged and grabbed him with enough leverage to hold him until the other officers could rush in to help. The Anderson police took him into custody and he received the help he needed. I hope he is doing well today. He was just a guy who needed time to figure things out and God again gave me a chance to give him a chance.

I could have left it to the city police. He could have taken me over with him. I didn't need to get involved, but I'm glad I did. God has a habit of putting people where others need them. Here too was an example of where I was able to use patience and my training (preparation) to ease out of a bad situation.

* * * * * *

Throughout my career I had to call upon the Lord for strength and to be courageous. Sometimes my life or the lives of others depended on my courage. I am only human and have my own fears I live with daily. This was one of those times.

My wife and I were house hunting. We had our two sons with us. I was off duty, but we were in my police car. I heard a call go out about a man on a roof of a house and the homeowner did not know him.

I was about a mile away when I responded to the call. I am not a real fan of heights, but I climbed up the ladder in an attempt to talk the man down. The man was on the roof preaching and proclaiming that he was God. I was pretty sure he wasn't.

I started talking to him. I prayed to God for strength and courage to deal with the situation. I wanted to get the man down, keep him from falling, and deal with my own fears.

It's a Job

My son, Kris, was observing all of this from the car. He asked his mother, "Why is Daddy sitting on the roof?"

With the courage and strength from God I was able to talk the man down and assisted him off the roof. I was also able to overcome my own fears to solve the problem.

* * * * * *

There was another time when I had to reach into that bag of courage. My son was riding with me on patrol that day. I tried to have all three of my sons ride with me at one time or another. I wanted to show them to be respectful of the law and to understand the job I did on a daily basis.

This particular night my youngest son was in the car with me. A dispatch came over the radio about a drunk driver. The dispatcher warned me that the driver had told his wife that he was planning to kill the first police officer who stopped him.

I located the vehicle and stopped it, praying to God for the courage (and wisdom) I would need to handle the situation. When I approached the driver's side of the car, he started yelling at me and tried to grab me. I pulled him out of his car through the driver's window, handcuffed him, and took him to the Madison County jail to take a breathalyzer test.

On the way to the jail I heard a call for a pursuit up towards the Frankton area. I dropped the prisoner off at the jail and started towards the pursuit. I asked God for a different type of courage and strength.

Because I had my son with me I had to help in the pursuit but yet not put him in danger. It was a moment when I had to use fear as a tool. I had to respect the danger I could have put my son in if I had been more aggressive. This is also true for the public in general. There are times when we have to back off to keep the situation from going out of control and hurting a crowd of people. While my particular car may not get the bad guy, it's for darn sure he will never outrun a police radio.

When we got close to the pursuit, I passed the car being chased. Usually I would have rammed the car but I did not. I had three opportunities to do so but I did not. The man was eventually caught in Tipton County.

There are other times when the situation is more straightforward. I was going to the store to get some money for my sons who both had dates. While on my way to the store to cash a check I overheard a pursuit coming towards me.

I jumped in the pursuit, even though I was off duty. We chased the car around the Chesterfield, Indiana area. There were two occupants in the vehicle. We surrounded the car just north of Chesterfield. I literally pulled the passenger through his window onto the ground. It made a fast and firm impression, and both men were arrested without incident.

I tell people that I do these things without thinking but that is not entirely true. I have my police training that helps me to react to a situation properly and decisively. I also prepare myself daily through prayer. God gives me the courage and strength to do whatever I am called to do in my profession. All I have to do is ask. My prayers are answered in God's perfect timing.

* * * * * *

Not all crimes are committed by the stereotypes we see on TV shows. A serious crime can be committed by a person in scrubs or a first rate suit just as well as a guy in a hoodie.

I was called over to Prosecutor William Lawler's office. He showed me a news article where two women were going to sue a local doctor for aborting their babies. He asked me to work the case.

I interviewed the two women and later identified a third victim. I took their statements and interviewed many more patients that accused the doctor of numerous offenses. I even interviewed the doctor with his attorney present.

He told me he had never performed an abortion or believed in abortions. He also told me that he had never recommended to any of his patients to get an abortion.

It's a Job

William Lawler, deputy prosecutor James Nave, and I went to Indianapolis. We went to an abortion clinic. They knew the doctor and showed us the files of his patients who had received abortions.

The doctor was arrested. We went to trial and the jury convicted him on three illegal abortions. He was sentenced to the department of corrections for 24 years with 8 years suspended.

I then went to the medical licensing board and filed a complaint. Then I testified and the doctor's medical license was taken away from him. After his conviction I received this note from one of the victims:

To whom it may concern:

I am writing to say thank you to the Madison County Police Dept. for all the hard work they did in the (doctor's) case. Being one of the victims, words cannot express my appreciation to everyone involved in the investigation and successful prosecution of a man who thought he was above the law. A terrible injustice was done and had it not been for the dedication, loyalty and professionalism of Detective Sam Hanna, the outcome could have been quite different. I am thankful that an injustice was righted in the eyes of the law. I will forever be grateful to Detective Sam Hanna for the tenderness, compassion, and kindness he showed me in what turned out to be one of the most traumatic times in my life.

Thank you
One of (the doctor's) *victims*

* * * * * *

Here is another case of where a doctor's lack of pride in respecting their commission caused serious harm. A physician who abuses their prescription writing trust can do a lot of damage. It's a serious crime that can take a person's life. We've all seen the results in the situations with "celebrity doctors" and the early deaths of their famous patients.

On October 17, 1983 I received a phone call from St. Vincent Hospital in Indianapolis. I was told there was a female victim there from Madison County. She was thought to be a victim of adult abuse. The woman had been admitted into the hospital. Her entire body was covered with lesions. She was incoherent, had received an overdose of drugs, and was near death.

I went to the hospital to interview her and was told that she was a nurse for a local Madison County doctor. She said she worked for the doctor and that they were special friends.

I checked with local pharmacies and found the nurse had been written several prescriptions by her boss and friend. There were numerous pharmacies that had been used.

I interviewed the doctor. She was not very helpful. Several months of investigative work followed which involved the Attorney General's office, the Federal Drug Enforcement Administration, St. John's Hospital, the Indiana Medical Licensing Board and others. Based on the investigation, the Indiana Medical Licensing Board issued an "Emergency Suspension" of the doctor's license, which barred her from practicing medicine in Indiana for 90 days. The doctor did not bother to come to the hearing. Her license was permanently taken away at follow up hearing.

* * * * * *

It may be even worse when a person who is trained to represent the law succumbs to temptation and violates the legal rights of someone who has placed their trust in them.

I had a case where a lady came in and filed a complaint against a local attorney who had also once been the Madison County Prosecutor. She accused him of taking money from her to invest. She said she did not know what he did with the money but it was not invested. The victim had major health issues that may have taken her life and she had been saving the money for her son's college education.

I asked the accused attorney to come in. He was read his Miranda Rights and he waived them. He then admitted to taking the money and misusing it.

It's a Job

I spoke with Prosecutor Rodney Cummings. I told him what my case was and the admissions the attorney had made.

The State charged the attorney with one count of Class C felony theft, two counts of Class D felony theft, and one count of Class C felony corrupt business influence. On July 9, 2001, the attorney plead guilty to all four counts. On August 29, 2001, the trial court sentenced him as follows: 14 years for the three theft counts and 8 years corrupt business influence to run consecutive with the 14 years. He also was ordered by the court to refund the money he had been entrusted with.

* * * * * *

People in positions of authority have an obligation to honor that authority. When they abuse their position we get involved.

Detective Dennis Maxey worked a case where a man had two antique cars that had been stolen. He identified the son of the victim as a suspect. We interviewed the high school student and he admitted to stealing the cars, but he also implicated an Anderson High School teacher in the theft with him.

The teacher was an antique collector. He had driven the student to his house and the cars were taken without the owner's permission. With the juvenile's parents' permission we wired the juvenile and sent him in to talk to the teacher so we could listen as they talked about the theft.

We later went to the school and spoke with the teacher in the principal's office. He was interviewed and initially denied things until we played the tape. He admitted what he had done but played it off.

He was arrested. There was a conviction and a suspended sentence. I went to the licensing board and his teacher's license was suspended by the state of Indiana.

Police work is one job where a person can really make a difference in another person's life. I can't say enough for the good training and mentoring I received to do my job. I also believe that God has put me where I need to be to do His work. God used me in each of these situations.

It's a Job

* * * * * *

Still there are situations that go beyond human comprehension. You can't let them overcome you, but you can't avoid being struck by your inability to understand that most troubling of questions – "Why?"

In my 38 years with the Madison County Sheriff's Department I have seen and investigated cases that were heart wrenching. If it had not been for my children and God giving me the strength to deal with these cases I do not know what I would of done.

In November of 1992 a stepmother was asleep in her trailer while her toddler stepdaughter played out in the front yard. The little girl played with broken glass with jagged edges. She fell on a piece of glass and it punctured her juggler vein.

When we arrived at the trailer we saw the little girl lying on the ground by the trailer. There was a blood trail leading to the door of the trailer. I observed her little bloody hand prints on the door. It really broke my heart.

I ended up arresting the stepmother for Neglect of a Dependent. She was adjudicated guilty. The Judge sentenced her to probation and she had to pick up glass in the Anderson City parks.

* * * * * *

There was a murder suicide I worked. A man had killed his wife who was critically ill. He shot his dog then killed himself. In one sense I could justify what was going through the man's mind. I understood it, yet I did not. I had to ask God for clarification.

* * * * * *

I was also the lead investigator of a suicide and triple homicide near Frankton, Indiana. The husband first shot his wife in the kitchen. He shot his son while he slept in his bed. He then shot and killed his daughter in the hallway. After committing the murders, the man went in to his bedroom and called the Madison County dispatcher. He told her what he had done. He then shot and killed himself.

It's a Job

I kept asking myself how a man could kill his family. No matter how you looked at it, it was wrong. I did not care what problems the parents might have had. It didn't give anyone the right to kill another person – let alone your family. It also troubled me that he had forced the dispatcher to go through the trauma of hearing a man shoot himself.

I remember going home and it was a cold wet night. I got home and I remember lying in bed asking God "Why?" I remembered learning that God taught in the Bible that this is not a perfect world and there would be pain. He also promised he would be with us. I wonder if God understands why we are the way we are. I guess it's like two old men sitting on a park bench and wondering why the world is so messed up. One might not be able to explain it to the other, but it's better than sitting alone.

* * * * * *

I worked another case where a man was at home with his wife and daughter-in-law. He received a call from his son that he was coming over to kill all three of them. The dad got his gun for protection.

A little later a noise was heard in the garage. The father went out and confronted his son who was armed, and who was also wearing a hockey goalie's mask.

The father had to kill his son to protect his wife, daughter-in-law, and himself. When we arrived he was devastated.

The prosecutor looked at the case. It was ruled a case of self defense and no charges were filed.

I felt so bad for the father. I then remembered this verse from Luke 10:19 – *Behold, I have given you authority to tread on serpents and scorpions, and over all the power of the enemy, and nothing shall hurt you.* (ESV)

I also thought of this one:

Matthew 5:4 says *"Blessed are those who mourn, for they shall be comforted."* (ESV)

It's a Job

I put myself in the place of that father and I didn't like the way it hurt.

* * * * * *

During my career in law enforcement one of the worst things I had to do was to make a death notification. I always remembered what Sheriff John Gunter taught me about treating people with compassion and dignity. He also encouraged us to speak to people the way we would like to be told of these things.

I recall an accident where two brothers were in a car that went off the road and turned upside down in the water. I joined with several other officers and firemen who tried and were unsuccessful in saving the brothers. When we identified them I went and notified the family. My heart hurt for the family.

* * * * * *

There was another family where both of their sons committed suicide. One had shot himself, and the other, several years later, died of carbon monoxide poisoning. I was sent in both cases to find them. I did not know how to tell the family. I prayed and God gave me the words, but they were still hard to say.

I found another young man who had killed himself – a senseless death. I kept asking myself why someone so young would have a reason to kill himself. His parents were wonderful people.

* * * * * *

Shortly after my oldest son had died in a traffic accident, I helped to investigate two fatal accidents where high school students were killed. When I went to talk to the parents I tried to be very compassionate.

The one boy had died when the car he was driving was hit by a train. The young man had skipped school to go play golf during graduation week.

His brother had been involved a car-train accident about a year before. He was hurt and his girlfriend was killed. I knew their mom. She was a manager of a local restaurant and was an

66

awesome lady. When I went to make the notification I saw the graduation invitations on the dining room table. My heart sank. I asked God for the words because I had none to say to the family. I was sick.

In the second accident another high school student wrecked on her way to school one morning and was killed. I knew her dad. Back in the day I had arrested him several times. He had turned his life around and he and his wife were wonderful parents.

I went to talk to him after the accident and later that night my wife and went to their house to give what comfort we could. I had been there but did not know what to say. I had once arrested this man but now I wept for him and his family. That in itself was a lesson on how people and situations can change. He and his family became some of our closest friends – friends of the heart.

* * * * * *

I've been used by God to help comfort these families and many more throughout my career with the Madison County Sheriff's Department. These situations were hard but God blessed me with the chance to be an ambassador of his love. In another situation I was given that gift.

I had been told about my own son's death by Captain Randy Simmons. He had been a friend for a long time and was very respectful. That had to be an awful moment for Randy. Not only was he delivering the bad news to the parents, he was also delivering the bad news to a friend and co-worker. While I will always remember the hurt of that moment, I will also always be thankful for Randy and the way he handled that situation.

Over those 38 years I have been asked how I have dealt with seeing these tragedies. I tell people that I prayed constantly. I also went home at night, put on my gym shorts, and sat on the floor with my boys to play with matchbox cars, or I coached them in baseball or football. My grandmother Sitto was right when she spoke of the importance of family.

My Grandmother Sitto

My parents

Dad (on patrol) at Frisch's

Sam with his friend, first sheriff, and mentor John Gunter

Our sons - from left to right Matt and Ashley Hanna - Mary Lawrence Phillips and Andrew Hanna

Lori and Sam with sons (L to R) Andrew, Matt, and Kris

Chapter 8

Oh, What a Tangled Web

If we confess our sins, he is faithful and just to forgive us our sins and to cleanse us from all unrighteousness. – 1 John 1:9 (KJV)

People can get themselves in an awful mess. Then they do something to try to cover up the crime and it always gets worse.

On the early morning of November 10, 1987 I was called out. There had been a murder and an attempted murder in Frankton, Indiana. I went to the residence and met Randy Simmons who was the supervisor of the investigations division.

A woman had been strangled with her own sweat shirt. She was dead in the garage area. The assailant had tried to strangle the woman's daughter with a telephone cord. She was a teenager and was able to get away.

She ran to a neighbor's house for help. When we arrived she told us the man who had killed her mom and tried to kill her was a man her mom had been dating. Her mom had met him at a gas station in Marion County Indiana.

She told us his name and we located an address for him. We requested authorities in Marion County to check his residence. We were later notified he had been picked up and was in the jail in Indianapolis, Indiana.

Randy Simmons and I went to the location where the suspect was being held. We went in to the location and before we left I read him his Miranda Rights.

We left the detention facility. While we were on our way back to the Madison County jail I started talking to him about his activities earlier in the morning. Before we got back to the jail, in Anderson, Indiana, the suspect admitted to me that he had killed his girlfriend and he had tried to kill her daughter.

He said they had met in Indianapolis at a gas station where he worked and they started dating. She did not know he was married.

They got into an argument and he strangled her with her sweatshirt. He told us that her daughter woke up and he panicked and tried to kill her because she could identify him.

When we got back to the Madison County jail he gave a taped statement after being read his rights again. He was formally charged with Murder and Attempted Murder. He ended up pleading guilty and was sentenced to 40 years for the Murder and 30 years for Attempted Murder.

I've thought about how that man would be free today if he had not cheated on his wife. If the two would have pulled back from their argument and one of them had just walked out of the house the woman would be alive today. Then he compounded his sentence by attempting to kill the girl.

If I had a time machine I wouldn't go back for the glory of arresting that guy. I would go back to get a job working with him in that gas station so I could have grabbed him by the collar and said, "What is wrong with you, buddy? You're a married man!"

* * * * * *

Even a person who knows the law can be foolish enough to commit a crime.

On October 4, 1994 the Flair Design Limited factory was destroyed by fire in Alexandria, Indiana. The Alexandria Fire Department fought the fire. They were assisted by surrounding fire departments. A fireman was injured while he assisted to extinguish the fire.

The initial investigation determined it was an Arson fire. During the investigation the arson inspector found a pair of gloves and a kerosene lantern.

Prior to May 22, 1997 the FBI received a tip on who had started the fire. In a meeting prior to arresting the suspect we discussed the fact that the arsonist was a civilian jail officer of the Madison County Police Department and, at the time he set the fire, he was working as a reserve police officer for the Alexandria Police Department.

Oh, What a Tangled Web

We decided on the morning of May 22, 1997 we would pick up the arson suspect and also have on hand the full time Alexandria Police officer the suspect had been working with the night of the fire. Randy Simmons, who was my supervisor, assigned me to locate and pick up the arsonist. He also said I would be the one to question him.

Later in the morning of May 22, 1997 Randy Simmons determined where the suspect was located and who he was with. I called Kent Wilson, the man who was with our suspect. I knew Kent because he too had once worked at the Madison County jail and now was a police officer just north of Madison County.

I told him we wanted to talk with his passenger. We discussed where we would meet. I then told Kent that when he saw us there he was to take the suspect's weapon and truck keys and get out of the vehicle.

When we got to the location Kent did as I had told him. Then Randy Simmons and I took the suspect into custody. Kent told us the suspect had figured out what was going on and wanted the truck keys and his weapon. He said he was scared and jumped out of the truck when he saw us.

The arson suspect was read his rights. Between the time we had left the area where they had been fishing near Marion, Indiana and we got to the Madison County Sheriff's Department, the suspect confessed to the arson. He was then read his rights again at the Madison County Sheriff's department and he signed a waiver.

In his taped statement he said the gloves found at the scene had been issued to him by the Alexandria Police Department. The kerosene lamp came from his grandmother's house. He not only admitted to setting the arson fire but he also said he had committed a robbery of a financial institution in Elwood, Indiana.

He was charged with the Arson which was a Class A felony since a fireman had been injured fighting the fire. He was not charged with the robbery because it was past the Statute of Limitations. He plead guilty and was sentenced to the Department of Corrections.

71

Oh, What a Tangled Web

I later received this note from Kent Wilson:

May 22, 1997 is a day that I won't soon forget, as I actually replay the events over in my mind quite often and thank God it turned out the way it did. I had only been on the police department for a little over a year and a friend from my previous employer and I had planned on going fishing at Mississinewa Reservoir. When we got to the reservoir, my friend said he didn't have a fishing license, so we got one at the bait shop. The funny thing is, he had just said "I don't want to be looking over my shoulder all day," little did I know, that statement set the tone for the day.

Shortly after getting the license and the start of our fishing, I received a page to call the Madison County Sheriff Department. When I called, I spoke with Sergeant Harp who asked where I was and who I was with. I told him I was fishing with a friend and at the reservoir. It was just a few minutes after speaking with Sergeant Harp, that I received a page to call Detective Sam Hanna. When I called and talked to Sam, he also asked where my friend and I were fishing and if we would meet him someplace, as he needed to talk. We agreed to meet at Oak Hill High School and I told him we would be in a red Chevy 4x4.

On the way to meet Detective Hanna, my friend kept rocking back and forth in the passenger seat, rubbing his rosary beads and making comments about "If they try to arrest me, we will run or fight them." I asked if he had done something wrong, as I had my off duty weapon in the truck between us. As he said no, I was taking the gun from between us and sliding it down in my driver side door.

As we got to Oak Hill, I kept talking to my friend and told him maybe something happened and they need to get you to family. I did this as a distraction because, quite frankly, I had no clue what was about to take place. When Sam and Detective Randy Simmons pulled up, we both got out of the truck and instantly put our hands on the bedside. My friend kept saying what's going on and I kept telling him to just do what he was told to do and everything would be alright.

Oh, What a Tangled Web

Once my friend was handcuffed and secured in the detective car, I was told I could take my hands off the truck and to relax, as they didn't want me, rather my friend. When I asked what happened, never in my mind, did I expect to hear what I heard. What I heard was that my friend had committed a multi-million dollar arson, while in police uniform and working in police capacity. If that wasn't bad enough, I was also informed of an armed robbery of a credit union a few years earlier.

Although Sam didn't tell me what was going on this particular day, I knew it was something major. I could tell in his voice. I believe Sam didn't tell me, not because of not trusting me, rather he knew the background of my friend being experienced in martial arts.

Given the events of May 22, 1997, I have the utmost respect for Sam. Both Sam and Randy treated me with professionalism and respect. You have no idea how much I reflect back on that day and often thank God it didn't turn out bad for any of us. That has and will stick with me for the rest of my days. I firmly believe it was due to the calmness and professionalism shown by Sam on this particular day it turned out to where nobody got hurt or even worse. I don't think Sam could've done anything different, as the situation turned out safely and nobody got hurt.

In both of these cases the suspects admitted what they had done. In obtaining the confessions I tried to meet each person on their level and treat them with respect. I always hoped that by getting the suspects to confess they could, in some way, meet God on God's terms and seek to be forgiven for whatever crime they may have committed.

* * * * * *

Still people continue to compound their bad choices.

On March 5, 2001, a woman shot and killed her husband while he slept in their Madison County home. After her attempt to dispose of his body failed, she drove off with the couple's child.

A passerby stopped to aid the woman whose car was parked on the side of a Michigan road with "help" written on a diaper in the

73

window. The wife of the victim asked for the police and initially told investigating officers that an African-American couple had broken into her home and abducted her and her son. She also asked the police to check on her husband.

I overheard the radio traffic while I was off duty but in my police car. I was taking Pastor Jim Lyon from our second service at North Anderson Church of God to the third service held at Madison Heights High School. I was called out and proceeded to the residence.

The residence was immaculate and small foot impressions were observed on the hardwood floor. I let the crime scene tell the story as to what happened and God gave me the wisdom to understand what it meant. I then asked Captain Randy Simmons if Detective Bob Blount could be called out. Bob and I then proceeded to Michigan.

We picked up the victim's wife and child at the Michigan State Police post. Detective Blount and I transported them back to the Madison County Sheriff's Department. There we arranged care for the child and later questioned the victim's wife.

She later admitted that she had killed her husband after being read her Miranda Rights. She told police that her husband had repeatedly asked her to do things in their relationship that she was not comfortable doing and that he had threatened to take their child away when she told him she had filed for divorce. She admitted to having taken the gun she had used to kill the victim from her grandparents' home because she wanted to be able to protect herself.

She said that she had shot her husband several hours after he had forced her to do things she did not want to do. I prepared a Probable Cause Affidavit that charged the suspect with murder. The jury found her guilty but mentally ill. The trial court imposed the maximum sentence of sixty-five years. She was sentenced to the Department of Corrections. Her sentence was later reduced to fifty-five years. It was a sad situation all the way around.

* * * * * *

Oh, What a Tangled Web

No crime remains silent. There is always some piece of evidence that will speak for the victim long after the screams and the shots go silent.

I had taken off work on April 23, 1998. I was called in to investigate a double homicide that had occurred just west of Alexandria, Indiana. Upon my arrival I observed bullet holes on the side of the trailer. Inside the trailer there was a man and a woman on the bed. They both had been shot and were dead.

I had no idea where to begin. I silently prayed to God for wisdom so as to give these two people justice. As I started to investigate what had happened, I learned that the woman's daughter had overheard her mom on the phone early in the morning. The daughter later heard gunshots. She called for her mother and found her and her male companion dead.

I visualized where and how the shooting took place. I remember thinking to myself that whoever did this had to be familiar with the layout of the bedroom. Whoever it was that did the shooting had shot blindly into the room hitting his targets.

As I investigated further, it came to our attention that the phone call had come from her ex-father-in-law's residence. Footprints in a garden had been found leading from the suspect's father's home to where the two people were killed. This is also where her ex-husband lived. We went in to talk to him. We woke him up. We also found the murder weapon underneath the bed where he was sleeping.

A trial was later held in Madison County Superior Court 1 where he was found guilty and sentenced to the Indiana Department of Corrections.

You would like to think that a person who goes to prison would serve his time and learn his lesson. Some people can't seem to learn anything.

In the early 1980s I was still in uniform. I covered a shooting where a man was shot on his front porch. It was thought initially to be a drive by shooting. I had a ballistics expert look at the scene. We determined that the shots had been fired from the field across the road.

My investigation showed that the shooter was a neighbor. They had been growing marijuana together and ended up having a dispute. The neighbor laid in the field across the road and shot the victim twice. Another bullet went into the side of the trailer and it just missed a baby asleep in a crib.

I tried to get enough evidence to arrest the neighbor but was unable to do so. I found that the shooter had a lengthy record and had also been told that, back in the sixties, he was a suspect in a murder. I contacted the A.T.F. Agent, James Quearry, and he agreed to help.

We sent an informant into the neighbor's home. They knew each other. The shooter had several guns; one of which was a sawed off shotgun. After being told of what was in the trailer, Agent Quearry and I had a plane fly us over the trailer for pictures and description for search warrant.

We served the search warrant. The shooter was charged with possession of marijuana, dealing in marijuana, possession of sawed off shotgun, and other gun charges. An enhancement was added because the shooter was a habitual offender.

There was a pretrial conference. The defendant, his attorney, the deputy prosecutor, and I attended. The attorney for the suspect said his client would take 6 years. I said, with his record, he would have to take 20 years, and the deputy prosecutor agreed. The defendant plead guilty and was sentenced to 20 years in prison. The habitual offender enhancement was dropped.

After the defendant did his time and was released from prison he moved back to his property. While he was living there he had a high powered rifle and was shooting it. While doing so, one of the projectiles traveled to a trailer south of his trailer.

The projectile went through the wall of the trailer. It traveled through the bathroom and almost hit a child on the toilet. I charged the defendant with Criminal Recklessness. He later plead guilty and was sentenced accordingly.

Oh, What a Tangled Web

As an officer of the law you can lead a man or woman to the waters of justice, but you can't always make them think.

Chapter 9

Facing the System

There are six things that the Lord hates, seven that are an abomination to him: haughty eyes, a lying tongue, and hands that shed innocent blood, a heart that devises wicked plans, feet that make haste to run to evil, a false witness who breathes out lies, and one who sows discord among brothers. – Proverbs 6:16-19 (ESV)

The job of a law enforcement officer would be much easier if witnesses would cooperate, if everyone would tell the truth, and if you didn't have to face the many legal technicalities an officer faces today. All of this is a part of the process and, in some cases, a good counterbalance to ensure that justice is served and the rights of the accused are protected. Still it is something an officer must face and they must be able to make their reasoning stay on top of their emotions.

I had not been a detective very long when we started having burglaries on the eastside of Madison County. The phone lines were cut on the residences. That was the only thing the burglaries had in common.

I had heard there was a man in the Madison County jail that was a known fence of stolen property. I had no other idea how to solve theses burglaries but to try to get this man to talk with me. I got him out and said to him that he owed me nothing and I owed him nothing. In fact we did not even know each other personally. That was the first step. You can't expect a person to be honest with you if you are not honest with them.

He said that he had nothing to say to me and he wanted to go back to his cell. I put him back, but I prayed that he might have a change of heart. It is easy to think that a criminal is all bad and that he doesn't have a heart, let alone the possibility of a change of heart. A little bit of common respect is rare to most men and women caught up in crime. They expect to be treated with loathing. They don't always respond to that common respect, but when you begin to establish yourself as a stand up guy it can open some doors. A couple of weeks later he sent word out he wanted to talk with me.

The fence told me of a man who was a known burglar and who had just beaten his girlfriend. He said this girl and the burglar had dated for some time. He said if anyone would know about the burglaries it would be her.

I took an Anderson city detective with me and we went to talk with her. She had bandages all over her but would not say who beat her. She refused to talk with us. I took the officer back to the Anderson City Police Department. When I arrived on station, Randy Simmons told me the lady had called and said that if I came back, by myself, she would talk to me.

I went back to talk with her. She told me who had beaten her and that he was the one committing the burglaries. She even admitted to doing a burglary with him. As we talked she told me of three other men who committed burglaries with him as well. She said she would not talk to me before because her ex-boyfriend was connected to an Anderson city detective.

I found one of the men she told me about in Anderson. He confirmed what she had said. He then went with Randy Simmons and me to Bowling Green, Kentucky where he showed us where the brothers lived. No one was home. As we were leaving we found one of the brothers walking a dog in the neighborhood. I told him that he and his brother needed to be in Anderson in two days. They took it to heart and hitchhiked all the way back to Anderson arriving in time.

They confirmed the information I already knew. They took me around and showed me all the places they had broken into with my main suspect. They helped me to retrieve some stolen property. I had been told of my suspect staying at a local motel on the night of one of the burglaries.

My suspect denied being in town during the time of the burglary. I went to the motel and got the registration for the room. A handwriting expert matched the motel registry to my suspect's signature.

Facing the System

During my investigation I learned of two Anderson City Policemen who were friends with my main suspect. I started asking questions about the relationship. One morning the two policemen visited me and told me I was barking up the wrong tree. One of the officers later sued me for a million dollars in a Delaware County court.

The lawsuit was later thrown out. I disregarded the threats from the two officers and the lawsuit. Those were just side issues and a waste of emotional energy. God gave me the wisdom to stay focused on what was important.

One of the officers, who was a supervisor in the Anderson City Police Department detective division, assigned an officer to talk with my suspect. Promises were made to my suspect without my knowledge. The suspect was charged with numerous burglaries and a battery on his ex-girlfriend. There was also a sentence enhancement Habitual Criminal charge filed as well.

Because of the promises made it negated the Habitual Criminal sentence enhancement. I was upset, but I remember the judge telling me not to worry about the sentence or the scales of justice. My suspect was sentenced to 40 years in the department of corrections.

Losing that Habitual Criminal sentence had had little effect on the outcome of his prison term, but, in another case, a sudden change in the testimony made a big difference.

* * * * * *

I've often wondered during my career in law enforcement why a person would commit a crime, be bonded out or be placed on probation, and then go out and commit the same offense. This really bothered me. There was the case of a young man I arrested, several years before I retired, that confused me.

I was investigating a residential burglary and was given a possible suspect's name. As I looked into his background I learned of an alias that he would sometimes use.

I got a phone call one day telling me where my suspect was located and I went to the residence on the southwest side of

Facing the System

Anderson, Indiana. As I parked my police car and got out I saw a young man walking down the driveway. I did not know what my suspect looked like but I asked him his name. He gave me the name of the alias I had been told about.

I told him he was under arrest. As I went to handcuff him he pulled away from me and then he swung at me. I shoved him into the side of my car. We then went to the ground wrestling, but I got him secured and handcuffed. I put him in the back seat of my car and started to take him to my office at the Madison County Police Department. In hindsight I know I should have had back up with me.

As we were going to my office, the suspect was kicking the back of my seat and popped his seatbelt lose. He then started trying to kick me in the back of my head. As I drove past an Anderson City Police car, the officer turned around and started following me. He must have seen the problem I was having because he waved me over to the side of the street. He jumped into the back seat with the suspect and rode the rest of the way with me to the Sheriff's Department.

We took him up to the interrogation room to question him. Another detective and I took the handcuffs off of him and read him his rights and when I asked him to sign his Miranda Rights Waiver he started yelling and jumped under the table in the room. It took six of us to carry him over to the jail.

He got out of jail after his court appearance. I continued working the case and did not hear anything about him – well at least I did not hear about him until sometime later.

I got called out one night to investigate a burglary at the Killbuck Golf Course. I finished processing the scene and was going home when I heard another officer being sent to another burglary of a residence. I met with him and investigated this burglary and ended up developing two suspects. One was a young African American. I located him and he identified the man with him as the same suspect I had arrested for the prior burglary – the one I had to wrestle with to get him handcuffed. The young African American told me where he had just dropped him off.

Facing the System

I went with several other officers to the residence. When we arrived I saw the same man I had arrested before. He started to walk away from me and I drew my weapon and pointed it at him and told him to stop

He turned around and started walking at me in a fast pace saying "SHOOT ME M____ F____" very loud numerous times. As he got closer I was trying to decide what to do. I did not want to shoot him, yet I did not want him to get away either.

I asked God what to do. I had just decided to try to grab him when another Madison County officer by the name of John Coogan tackled him. Again it took several of us to subdue him and get him handcuffed. I was very grateful that John Coogan did what he did.

In our daily life we have to make tough decisions in a split second. You just do not have time to think things through because they happen so fast. I went to work every day not knowing what the day might hold for me. I gave it to God.

When a man is out on bond, or is on probation, there is a good chance a suspect like the man I arrested would have to do consecutive time instead of concurrent time. I did not understand this either but did my job and again gave it to God.

* * * * * *

On September 20, 1986 a 21-year-old woman, living in Alexandria, Indiana, disappeared from her apartment. Seventeen days later, following an anonymous tip, I found her decomposed body along county road 1000 North in Madison County. Her identification was made through dental records.

I could not believe that one human being could do this to another. As I started my investigation I was told many rumors, and everyone pointed fingers at each other. I tried to follow her steps of the early morning in which she disappeared.

My investigation pointed towards her boyfriend at the time. He was arrested in connection with her death along with one of his friends. A man had come forward who lived in an apartment on the eastside of the victim's apartment.

He said he had heard her scream. He then looked out the window that looked down in the 21-year-old's apartment. He said he saw the victim hit by her boyfriend. I went to window and looked down on the victim's apartment and I saw the area the witness described.

I arrested the boyfriend for the murder. As Randy Simmons and I walked him over to the Madison County Jail from the administration part of the building he tried to bolt out the front door. We subdued him and had him booked into jail. His friend was arrested as well.

An attorney was appointed for the boyfriend. The attorney hired an investigator to question witnesses. When the investigator questioned the witness who said he had seen the murder he was intimidated and changed his story. He said he had not told the truth.

Charges against both were later dropped as a result of insufficient evidence. The prosecutor said it was not clear if the witness had seen what he said he had seen. He said, since the witness changed his story, the man would not be a good witness.

I continued my investigation and the leads kept ending up in a dead-end. The rumors got worse and it was hard to tell what was true and what was a false. Because the witness said he had not told the truth the case has gone unsolved.

This last case highlights where ignorance of the law overcame justice.

It was around June 14, 1991. A mother of two was reported missing by her family to the Madison County Police department. We were told by her husband she had left for work and had never come home. She worked in Marion County at C.I.C. Enterprises.

I put out a dispatch about the missing woman and the vehicle she would have been driving. Her car was found in a parking lot of a hospital in Marion County, near the Castleton, Indiana exit. It had been found by Marion County authorities. It was towed back to Madison County and was processed.

Facing the System

When we searched the house, the missing woman's sweater was still there. Her sister, who worked where her sister did, said she always took the sweater because the office where they worked was always cold. We continued to search the house and really did not find anything.

I contacted an expert on blood out of Florida. We had him come to Indiana and, with a court order, we searched the house again. Using Luminal, the expert found what he thought might have been blood in an area that had been cleaned on the carpet.

As time went by I was contacted by the Indianapolis television station Channel 13. They told me that a lady had called but did not identify herself. She said she knew who had killed the missing lady but hung up before she gave any facts.

As my investigation continued it was revealed that, since his wife had been missing, her husband had a girlfriend. I tracked down an accident report related to the missing woman's husband. He had been involved in an accident in Brown County, Indiana. His girlfriend had been listed as a witness.

I located a factory where she worked that was located near downtown Indianapolis. I went there and asked to speak to her. When she came into the room and saw me she started crying and said she knew I was investigating her ex-boyfriend's missing wife.

She told me she had been the one who called Channel 13 news. She then went on to tell me how her boyfriend admitted to killing his wife and disposing of the body. The husband was arrested after it was determined by the prosecutor there was enough evidence to do so.

The case finally went to trial, even though the body was never found. The ex-girlfriend testified as to what she had told me. She became emotional on the stand but was consistent with what she had said.

The jury found the suspect innocent. They later said they thought the girlfriend was just an angry ex-girlfriend, and alluded that they thought she had lied. They also said they would have felt better about a conviction if we had found a body. Without a body, how could they be absolutely sure a crime had been committed?

After the trial was over we talked to the jury. What bothered me most was that some members of the jury had told the other jurors that you can retry him if we found the body. The prosecutor and I both explained to them that we couldn't retry the man because of the double jeopardy rule that states that a defendant can't be retried for the same offense after a decision has been made.

These last two cases have bothered me throughout my career as an investigator and police officer. In the first case a witness changed his testimony and said he had lied. In the second case the jury thought a witness had lied and they believed that the man could be tried again after the body was found.

It wasn't about me personally winning or losing. In both cases the victim's families failed to get closure or justice. It is a bitter pill to swallow, but sometimes you have to do so. You can't let it rule you, but it should bother you. That thirst for justice and your compassion for the victims is the foundation of why you do this job. Sometimes the only satisfaction is knowing that God will have the final say.

<u>Chapter 10</u>

The End of the Rope

Do not be a fool–why die before your time? – Ecclesiastes 7:17
(NIV)

It is painful to think of all of the people in this world who think
they are at the end of their rope. As a law officer we can only do
what we can. I've mentioned the man who threatened to jump off
the bridge. I was glad that had a good ending. Here are some
other examples of human desperation.

In the late 1970s the Madison County Police Department had
investigated numerous burglaries in the Elwood, Indiana area.
There were not many leads. My wife was in nursing school and
working, so I would work a lot of my off time investigating these
crimes.

I was working midnights at the time and had stopped at the
Elwood Police Department. At that time they had several holding
cells. I asked one of the officers who they had in jail and he told
me. I was familiar with one of them, so I took him aside and
asked him if he knew who was doing the burglaries in the area.
He said he did not.

The other man in the young man's cell asked to talk to me. He
told me that the man that I had just talked to had been bragging
about doing burglaries in the area.

I again took the young man from his cell and confronted him
about the burglaries. Again he denied any knowledge of the
crimes. I told him I knew he was lying and he started crying and
admitted to doing the burglaries along with another young man
and two brothers. I ended up arresting all four of them; clearing
up numerous burglaries. All five confessed to their involvement.

Several weeks passed and I was on patrol. I received a radio
call and was told to go to the Elwood Police Department. Upon
my arrival I was told that one of the prisoners wanted to talk with
me. I spoke with him in one of the offices. It was the inmate that
had told me about his cellmate bragging about doing burglaries.

He had been arrested for stealing and cashing a social security check of one of his neighbors. He told me that his brother was in prison for a murder that had occurred in another county. In our conversation he kept saying he was afraid of going to prison.

I told him I could put a good word in with the prosecutor on his behalf because he had helped to clear up all those burglaries. Then he said he did not want to go to the Madison County jail.

He kept saying he was afraid the word would get out that he had helped me on a case. I told him I could have him put on as a trustee until the prosecutor could take a look at his case. He said he was concerned because the man who had shot me several months before was still in the Madison County jail and he was afraid of him. He seemed to be satisfied about being a trustee.

At the end of my shift at 8 a.m., I drove home and went to bed. Several hours later I received a phone call from a Madison County Sheriff's department jail officer. He told me that the man I had talked to earlier in the morning had hung himself at the Elwood Police Department in his holding cell.

It bothered me tremendously. He was a young man with a lot of years ahead of him. He had made a mistake and broke the law, but would have been treated fairly by the Criminal Justice System.

* * * * * *

This next incident really hit home.

I had a friend I had known since junior high school. My mom had worked for his dad shortly after she had married my dad and they had moved to Anderson. I went to high school with his sister. His brother had been a reserve police officer on the Madison County sheriff's department.

We had worked together at Community Hospital in Anderson, Indiana. He had been an orderly and I had worked as a security officer there as a part time job. I had the opinion that he was a good man.

The End of the Rope

He later owned several different businesses. He had made mistakes and had gotten into trouble. He was held accountable and built his business back up.

We would bump into each other once in a while. We would talk a little, but were not as close as we had been in the past. I did know he was working hard to help raise his children and send them to college.

Within a year or so of retiring from the Sheriff's department, I was working as a patrol officer on day shift. Captain Tim Davis contacted me and told me that my friend had killed himself by carbon monoxide poisoning. He said the reason he was contacting me is because my friend had left a note for the owner of the property where he had killed himself.

The note instructed the property owner not to go into the building where he had killed himself. He was to contact me and give me a second note he had written. In the second note my friend apologized to me. He wanted me to find him because he knew I would treat him with dignity.

I later found out that he had possibly made some mistakes that would cause him to be involved in the Criminal Justice system again. This bothered me because, no matter what trouble he was in, it was not worth him killing himself. My heart ached for his family.

No one should die before their time. He had had another brother die years before in an accident. The pain his family went through was not fair.

* * * * * *

Neither is it fair when a person commits "suicide by cop."

One night I had stopped home to eat supper. I had another officer riding with me. My captain called me and said that a man had called the Sheriff's department. He was threatening suicide. The captain thought that if I came out to talk with him he may not do it.

The End of the Rope

The officer with me and I went to the man's residence just north of Anderson, Indiana. I pulled up to the back of his house. He walked out of his house pointing a shotgun at my head threatening to kill me.

As he walked towards me yelling his threats I noticed his finger was not on the trigger. I kept trying to talk with him and he kept saying if I did not shoot him he was going to blast my head off.

As he got closer I holstered my weapon and jumped on him. We wrestled, and as I kept trying to get the shotgun from him, he kept asking why I did not kill him. It was apparent he was intoxicated.

I was able to get the weapon from him and handcuffed him. I then checked the weapon to unload it. There were no shells inside. He was then transported to the county jail.

He kept asking why I did not kill him. I asked him why his weapon was not loaded. He said he was aware of me and my reputation of being a tough cop. He said he could not kill himself but wanted me to do it.

I would have been justified that night if I had killed him. I was never in fear for my life. I was there to keep him from hurting himself. God protected all of us that night.

Maybe this is why I am eager to share my faith. The world is filled with so much desperation and my faith gives me so much hope.

Chapter 11

Iron Sharpens Iron

As iron sharpens iron, so one person sharpens another. –
Proverbs 27:17 (NIV)

It is true that "iron sharpens iron." Sometimes that "iron" is a
teacher, a coach, or a work mentor with whom you interact to
make you a better person than you were before. Sometimes that
"iron" is a bad turn in your health or your financial situation.
Whatever that "iron" is in your life it makes you stop in your
tracks to think about the path you are taking. Sometimes it gives
you the confidence to charge ahead. Sometimes you make a slight
correction in the way you do things. Sometimes it forces you to
become a completely different person.

* * * * * *

I've had people in my life who have sharpened me. In the
following example it was a subtle mistake I made in a case I was
working that made me a better officer.

In the late '70s a man was convicted for child molesting. He
was waiting to be sentenced when he filed for an appeal bond. It
was granted and he was released while he was awaiting the
decision on his appeal.

Several months later, around the 4th of July, I covered a
burglary in the area of Innisdale which is located on the west side
of Alexandria, Indiana. I was still a fairly green uniformed officer.
We usually worked our own cases.

As I worked the burglary, my investigation pointed to the man
who had just been convicted of child molestation and was out on
his appeal bond. I arrested him for committing the burglary. He
was brought to the Madison County Sheriff's Department.

I read him his Miranda Rights. I was familiar with the
landmark case *Miranda verses Arizona*. I had studied it in college
and again at the Indiana Law Enforcement Academy.

As I questioned the suspect in the burglary he requested an attorney. In accordance with the Miranda rules I did not ask him any more questions. Then I made a serious mistake.

As I was leaving the room to get a jail officer to take him back to his cell, I looked back at him and told him I did not understand why he would commit a burglary when he was out on an appeal bond.

He said when you're convicted of something you did not do, and you are going to prison, you might as well go ahead and break the law. All you can do at that stage is to shake your head and wonder what the world is becoming. I had him put into a cell. I then filled out my paper work and added what he had said.

My statement was not intended to be an official question. By responding to my comment it became a question asked after he had requested an attorney and therefore no longer permissible to use against him. By recording his response I made it a part of the evidence.

We went to trial and he was convicted of burglary. When I was on the stand I testified as to what he had said. In my mind I had made a statement and had not asked a question.

He appealed his conviction and the appellant court ordered a new trial. Fortunately the defendant decided to plead guilty instead of going to trial and he was resentenced.

God placed me in this job of being a police officer and making sure that people who violate the law will be held accountable. I also want to help young people make better choices and bring closure to victims. This is the purpose assigned to me.

I wasn't going to make that mistake again, but the lesson I learned helped me to become a better police officer.

I have taught the Introduction to Criminal Justice and Introduction to Criminology courses at Ivy Tech. I always used the experience in this case to help prepare future Criminal Justice workers. I want others to learn from my experience as I have worked as a police officer.

Iron Sharpens Iron

* * * * * *

Sometimes a bout of humility can keep a man sharp. Of all of my heroic deeds, I fear this will be the one my wife and my coworkers will remember most.

When pride comes, then comes disgrace, but with the humble is wisdom. – Proverbs 11:2 (ESV)

I was a detective on call one night when the Madison County dispatcher paged me and sent me just outside of Markleville, Indiana. It is located southeast of Anderson, Indiana.

I was told a lady had committed suicide. I went to the area and spoke with witnesses that lived nearby, and to her family. I called for the coroner and a deputy coroner was sent to the scene as well. Pictures of the scene were taken by the deputy coroner and me.

The deputy coroner determined the cause and origin of the death. It was determined to be a suicide. Evidence was collected and the scene was documented. So far this is a sad tale and I don't mean to make light of the situation, but what followed was a classic fear that many have had from time-to-time and I had to be one of the few to actually experience.

When taking pictures I had cut my finger on my camera. It was bleeding and I needed to put a bandage on it. I wrapped it with a handkerchief. That was all I had to work with.

When I left the area I stopped at a convenience store just west of Markleville. I parked right in front of the front door and walked in right to the cashier. I asked if he had any Band-Aids and he gave me two.

I stepped into the restroom next to the counter where I had spoken with the cashier to wash and dry my hand. I put the Band-Aids on and went to the restroom. Then I took off the coveralls I had on over my clothes. I was in the restroom for less than 5 minutes.

When I walked out of the restroom I saw the lights were off, the door to a freezer had been left ajar, and no one was in the building! I went to the front door and it was locked.

As I walked around I kept setting off the alarm. It became evident to me that I had been locked in and could not get out of the convenience store. I found the telephone and called the Madison County dispatcher to advise her of my situation. Between her and I laughing at what had just happened, I asked that she send someone to help me and asked that she call the state police and advise them so that I would not be mistaken for a burglar.

I then called home to tell my wife why I was going to be detained for awhile. The phone kept cutting out as the alarm was going off. She too was laughing at my peculiar situation. What was funny was that she did not believe me at first until she heard the alarm go off and the phone go dead.

A Madison County officer arrived, and instead of asking what he could do to help, he started laughing and photographed me in my predicament. After he was able to compose himself, he said he would be back. He left for a few minutes and came back. I was told the owner was out of town and the town marshal was as well. They were thought to have the only keys to the building.

Another man came a few minutes later and when he saw the predicament I was in he excused himself and said he would return. He explained that he had, at one time, been on the Markleville Police Department for a while.

He came back with a handful of keys and tried them in the front door. One of them did work and he was able to unlock the front door to let me out.

I remember driving home and laughing at myself. Then I looked out my side window of my car. I said out loud "Okay, God, I know you wanted to get my attention." Being humbled is good for the soul.

To this day I laugh at that night. When I get too prideful I remember how God can and will humble me. God has his way of keeping me in check.

* * * * * *

Iron Sharpens Iron

I have definitely been "sharpened" by the great police training I have received, but some of those training episodes have also had their humorous moments.

There the time I was participating in a training session at the police academy. We were doing scenarios where we had recruit officers participate in the training. I was acting as a burglar and the officers came to arrest me.

Instead of surrounding the building the officers entered the building like ants going to a picnic. I snuck out the back and came up behind them and shot them with my revolver (with blanks). We then discussed the scenario and what was done right and wrong.

During one of the drills one of the recruits accidentally shot me with a shotgun filled with wadding and gunpowder. I had third degree burns on my left hand as I held it in front of my face. The wadding hit my right bicep causing a third degree burn.

The next day I went to the hospital because my wound was infected. I was admitted to the hospital for two days because I was septic. It was six months since I had been shot six times. That was sure a memory. I was also in the hospital on my 1st year wedding anniversary. I healed up from that incident and returned to work as an instructor at the Indiana Law Enforcement Academy.

It's one thing to be hurt in the line of duty. It's quite another to be hurt in training. I thank God that, through these incidents, he has provided me with the strength to return to work quickly each time. I'm also thankful that none of these injuries have slowed me down. As a matter a fact they made me more tenacious than ever.

* * * * * *

I can also say that my experiences with the people I have arrested and the people I have helped have "sharpened" me. Some of them have taught me that a person, given a reasonable amount of respect, really can change their lives for the good. The loved ones of the victims of crimes or accidents have taught me a level of grace that can't even be found in church. Certainly I have learned a level of humility from these experiences that have led me to be a better officer and a better man.

Most of all I have been "sharpened" by the men and women I have worked with in my police career.

I have had a wonderful and successful career with the Madison County Sheriff's department. My ego would like to take most of the credit for that success, but I cannot. First of all I give all the credit to God. It has been through him that I have been able to do what I have accomplished.

I am especially thankful to God for placing several people in my path to help me along the way. I have worked for and with some awesome people in the Criminal Justice field. They have helped to sharpen me as "Iron sharpens Iron."

First of all it was Sheriff John Gunter who hired me. He taught me that it takes a real man to be a Christian Police Officer. He was a great example for learning how to treat suspects and victims.

He would praise you if you did something right and help you to learn from your mistakes. He was not afraid to discipline you but always made it clear that to discipline someone is to guarantee the mistake will not happen again. He treated the men and women he led fairly and was consistent.

Another man I want to talk about is Captain Randy Simmons. We hired in together and I watched him work his way up in the ranks. I put in for rank several times but withdrew when I saw I was going to have to leave the investigations division. I felt as though that was where I best served the citizens of Madison County. Randy knew that and always treated me as an equal.

He was my supervisor in the investigations division. He made sure I got my work done but gave me the freedom to do what I needed to do to make sure a victim of a crime was given justice. When I needed to talk through a case he was my sounding board. He would sometimes just listen or would give suggestions.

He would help me on cases to find the suspect. Sometimes he made sure the crime scene was worked and evidence was collected and he would tell me to go find who was responsible. The best compliment he ever gave me is when he called me a Policeman's Policeman.

Another man who helped me to be a good police officer was Detective Bob Blount. He worked a lot of cases with me. We traveled to different parts of the state working on cases. We talked about cases and the strategy we would use to solve a case. I was usually the lead investigator of a case but I learned a lot from Bob. He helped me to sharpen my skills as an investigator.

Another Investigator I worked with was Detective David Callahan. He helped me to make sure my T's were crossed and my I's were dotted. When we worked a murder case together I went to find the suspect and he served the search warrant and found evidence that helped the crime make sense. David was another person who would listen as I would talk a case through. I would like to think we helped each other to sharpen our skills.

Tim Davis and I hired on the Sheriff's Department on the same day. We also were promoted to patrolmen at the same time. We worked the same shift together and when I went back on the road he was my captain.

When I left investigations and went back on the road it was a difficult time in my career. In my opinion it was a political move. I thought it was unfair.

God used Tim Davis to keep me focused and to stay positive. He encouraged me and stood behind me. We shared Bible verses.

Tim went through some difficult times as well. With God's help, I have been there for Tim. Our friendship is definitely an example of Iron Sharpening Iron.

I worked a case with Daryl McCormick. He was an Anderson City Police Department detective. My wife called us the Odd Couple because he did great paper work to keep us organized while I was the one who wrote notes on my hands. My job was to go after the suspect tenaciously. Considering that he was a younger officer I learned a lot from Daryl. He was a West Point graduate and worked in the intelligence division. He taught me about gangs and their graffiti. He helped to sharpen my skills.

Another officer who helped me to become a better police officer was Sergeant W.W. Harp. He taught me safety and how to be cautious. He was always willing to help me.

As I mentioned earlier Patrolman Mike McKain was one of the officers early in my career who helped me to sharpen my skills as a police officer. He showed me how to work, have fun, and serve the public. I learned a lot from Mike in a short period of time.

Dennis Maxey and I have worked together for 28 years. When I worked the road early in my career he rode with me when he was a jail officer. After he was promoted to patrolman we worked the same shift.

No matter what position I held on the Sheriff's Department, Dennis was one of my best friends who I could lean on for common sense. He would listen then he would give me solid information or an opinion based on common sense.

On the day I was shot we worked with several officers earlier in the day looking for three escaped prisoners from the Madison County jail. After they were located and put back in jail I stayed out to finish my shift.

After I was shot and called for help two Anderson city police officers arrived to the scene. It wasn't long before Dennis, his wife officer Doris Maxey, Sergeant Bill Harp, and Patrolman Randy Simmons arrived. Seeing Dennis arrive gave me peace.

Dennis and I have been friends for years. At one time he was appointed by a Sheriff to be Administrative assistant. He was always backing me and protecting me so I could do my job. He encouraged and supported me. He helped me to be the officer I had become because he believed in me and my faith.

I truly believe these men crossed my path because God had it in his plan for me. He knew I had to be sharpened in many ways to carry the job he wanted me to do. Each one of the men that I have mentioned had a particular purpose to help me to become the type of police officer I became.

* * * * * *

98

Iron Sharpens Iron

Isaiah 6:8 says *Then I heard the voice of the Lord saying, "Whom shall I send? And who will go for us?" And I said, "Here am I. Send me!"* (NIV)

This verse sums up my 38 year career with the Madison County Sheriff's department. From the time I was an intern until I retired I was the one to say "I will do that." God opened many doors for me to have an opportunity to serve my fellow man. I wanted to honor my God every day.

God has used me in so many ways. I have been a hardnosed police officer, a mentor for young men, compassionate towards victims, and a leader for my fellow officers through my work ethic. I have worked the cases hard to send men and women to prison. I have worked just as hard to help some to turn their lives around. Whatever I needed to do I always heard God say "Whom shall I send, and who will go the distance," and I said "Here I am Lord, use me."

There have been times I have been called upon to do work outside of my comfort zone. I have always been willing to step up and do whatever I have been called upon to do. I have always felt God at my side, not pushing or pulling but encouraging me.

Some people might say it was a miracle that I was shot six times at point blank range and survived. I like to think that God placed me in the middle of his miracle plan for his people and gave me the opportunity to make a difference in people's lives.

Again I don't say these things to brag. I truly want to teach every aspiring officer that these principles work in real life.

Most of all I want to say a sincere thank you to all police officers who find themselves in what appear to be thankless situations. There are plenty of people who do appreciate us and daily pray that God will bless all who protect and serve.

Chapter 12

Some Final Notes

The main purpose of writing this book wasn't to showcase my bravado. I wanted to show young officers that it takes more than a gun, a badge, a vest, and strong muscles to be a good police officer. Even the training isn't enough by itself. My success at becoming a "Top Cop" has come from observing five rules.

1. Listen to God

2. Be willing to lay down your life for your friends so as to protect them.

3. Treat the public as you would like to be treated.

4. Give everything you have to give victims closure and justice.

5. Be fair with the accused.

A short version would say – God 1st, Others 2nd, Self 3rd.

Listen to God – a lot of people don't believe in God these days. When I see the results of the people I have met and served and the timing and circumstances that brought us together I have to also see something greater. When I see the times I should have been killed and the miraculous healing my body has received I have to believe in a higher power. When I think of the number of times I could have used the word "coincidence" I realize that this could not have been just a coincidence. When I sense him at my side I know he is there. He has made me aware of so many things that my human side would have ignored. He has shown me a promise that has taken away any crippling fear and has taught me one of the most effective tools a law officer can have on hand – compassion.

Be willing to lay down your life for your friends so as to protect them – While I respect the fear of death and the natural reactions of someone in mortal danger, I have never let it paralyze me with fear. I would do anything to protect another human being and especially my fellow officers. When we were investigating that crime scene where the distraught father pointed the shotgun at us, I kept him trained on me. Not because I was brave, but to protect my fellow officers. It was not my bravery, but my willingness that gave me the mental strength to do that. No one is spared death, but we can overcome its power by being unwilling to let fear overcome us and by keeping others first.

<u>Treat the public as you would like to be treated</u> – Just as every Christian is the face of how others see Christians; every law officer is the face of how others see us. We can't take our problems and bad days out on the people who see us in public every day. Let's face it; it is hard to hide in a police uniform. If they see respect, compassion, and good cheer, that is how they will see a police officer. If they see us as angry, rude, or throwing our weight around – that too is how people will view police officers. It doesn't take a good officer long to realize that we need the public goodwill much more than they need us.

<u>Give everything you have to give victims closure and justice</u> – I wish I could have undone the violence committed against that little girl and her mother who were killed near Lapel, Indiana. I don't know of any case that has hit me harder. Imagine that father if we hadn't brought the perpetrator to justice. There is something to be said about closure. What if it was my wife and child? It doesn't matter if you hit a million brick walls. Their pain and, if you have any heart at all, your pain will never let up until you bring resolution to the case. It is usually the only thing a police officer can do, so why not give it your all.

There is another aspect to giving it your all. God, the giver of life, has placed numerous cases like this in my path. I feel like each time I work a case like this and bring closure for victims I am honoring God and his gift of life.

<u>Be fair with the accused</u> – In this country we profess that a person is innocent until proven guilty. Even after the conviction most people do not cease to be a human being. There are some people who are pure evil, but most of the people an officer will arrest are the victim of their own bad choices. To be sure they must pay for these bad choices. Some will continue to make bad choices all of their lives, but we can't expect anyone to reform if

we label them as lost. Did you ever make a mistake and later change your ways? How did it make you feel when people remembered your mistake and failed to recognize your change?

The man who called to warn me that he had been hired to kill me didn't do so because he liked me. He made that plain at the first of his call. Still I had a reputation for fair play and it was that reputation that he respected enough to save my life and the lives of my family and neighbors. It makes no sense to rub it in when a person is down. They will remember how you treated them and they will either harbor a grudge or give you the respect that you have earned.

One of my favorite Bible verses is from Galatians 5:24-26 – *Now those who belong to Christ have crucified the flesh with its passions and desires. If we live by the Spirit, let us also behave in accordance with the Spirit. Let us not become conceited, provoking one another, being jealous of one another.* (NET)

This verse really covers my career in police work. Because of God's blessing I have been very successful as a Criminal Investigator.

It could be very easy to be conceited. Take the credit of bringing closure to the victims of crimes. When I gave my life to Christ I came to realize my life was no longer about me. I know I am not perfect but I work hard every day to honor God.

God has blessed me with the wisdom, tenaciousness, and compassion to work these cases. I have been successful and have received publicity. It's kind of like a football player running a touchdown who then points to the heavens giving God the glory. There will always someone very jealous, but you can't let that keep you from giving it your all and doing the right thing.

In one captain's meeting the captains were asked to report on their shifts and divisions. When it came to my captain he went to report on the cases being worked and solved. He was told by the Sheriff running the meeting that he did not want to hear about "the great Sam Hanna." It did not matter if it was a high profile case or a low profile case I worked them all the same.

Some Final Notes

There was no reason for anyone to be jealous of me or my work. I was doing what I believed God wanted me to do. He provided me the tools with which to do these things.

As a police officer each day we are asked to deal with all kinds of situations. People being dealt with are overwhelmed with all types of emotions. In answering the call and dealing with these people we must work hard at not provoking them.

As a Christian, God has armed me with common sense, compassion, good decision making abilities, and the ability to talk to people. We need to treat people with respect. They are either a victim of the situation or of their own self worth and choices. By provoking them we victimize them and ourselves.

We cannot allow the suspect or victim of a crime to provoke us in law enforcement. We, as law enforcement officers, cannot provoke the suspect or the victim of a crime. If we commit either one of these violations the whole scene worsens and someone could likely be injured or killed.

We belong to God. We must take these passions and desires and give them to God. That's easier said than done. Being a police officer is tough and stressful. Think of God as your trusted partner. Let God handle these emotions and you do the rest of the job. I listen to God and know he is in control not me. I am his servant. It's easy to let the badge, the gun, and that authority go to your head. Always remember that first and foremost you are a servant. That's a good rule for anyone in authority.

As my grandmother Sitto said, family is everything. Remember to keep your work separate from your family and to be the kind of person in all walks of life that will make your family proud. I will close this account with two letters from my sons.

From my son Matthew Hanna:

From a very early age most of my memories lack overt concern for the life and wellbeing of my father given his profession. I don't think it is because of a lack of understanding of the dangers that his career was constantly one that posed many dangers to him, but rather it is more due to the talks I had with him continually throughout my childhood. Whenever I would hint at concern for his life as a police officer he was always very serious in reassuring me that every day he went to work he had one concern in mind and that was to make sure that he made it back home to our family.

Anyone who has spent much time around my father knows that he possesses an almost unshakable sense of sincerity. He could be so convincing that even after getting older and hearing of other police officers' families who suddenly lacked a patriarch because of the risks of the profession, my father could still always assure me that nothing short of divine intervention could take him from this world. Especially before my brothers and I were still too young to provide for ourselves.

I realize that most children, at some age, realize that their fathers are not perfect and especially in today's world I feel this often times happens too soon and too early for most to be able to truly process and work through the sense of disappointment and wanting that this realization can produce. I can however say that, to me, I have not yet had to face such a disappointment. I have thought many times about this, and while some will likely say that this is only because of my own naiveté, I know it is not from any lack on my part to realize that my father does have flaws for I am all too aware of this. However, I have been a witness too many times in my life to situations that would have literally crippled most people, but have passed over my father without any falter in his core beliefs. His beliefs include the inherent dignity of all people and the overwhelming need that seems to drive him from within that justice is always both worth fighting for and should with no exception be applied to everyone equally regardless of one's financial situation.

My father's beliefs have been developed almost in opposition to his lifelong experiences of constant setbacks. Those beliefs have remained strong even in the most extreme situations that include; being shot 6 times at point blank range, and having a bomb nearly planted on his police car in our driveway that would have, if set up accurately, initiated an explosion when my dad started his car to leave for work. Also witnessing acts by many of the murderers and rapists he arrested on an almost daily basis – that should shake anyone's beliefs and faith to their very core.

In spite of all of this, along with numerous others, particularly the death of my older brother Kris in 2004 when he was only 22-years-old, none of these were strong enough to move my father's almost spiritual need to help others selflessly and without expecting anything in return.

All of these things are the reason, that while most people have not been able to continually call their fathers their hero beyond childhood, I do not even hesitate, now at the age of 30, whenever I'm asked whom my hero is or who my most important role model is.

I have come to realize that anyone that spends considerable time with my father soon comes to this same conclusion. I do not now and have never had lots of things in common with my dad. We have very different interests and we have often taken fairly different paths in our lives in terms of our pursuits. Still, having come full circle and realizing later in my life how many times my father's life was truly in jeopardy throughout his career, and especially since passing through my teenage years, I've been often times awestruck by both how fragile life is and how easily it can be taken in an instant. Yet I still know that my father was able to live each day while still working for the Madison County Police department without fear or doubt of his ultimate purpose in life.

I continue to appreciate his unrepentant and total dedication to his family – to my family. I will consider myself very lucky one day if I am able, like he is now, to look back on the majority of my days on this earth and see myself as someone who did not shirk away from challenges and always went out of his way to pursue for justice for those who have been wronged in life and to demonstrate such a profound belief in the equality of everyone that I no longer have to constantly reflect on my daily life and no longer wish I had done more to demonstrate this to others.

As a history major and a lifelong student of some of the most important and influential people of the 20th century in the United States I constantly see and hear many similarities between my *father's beliefs and pursuits and those of Theodore Roosevelt. T.R. was often quoted as instructing both his children, constituents, and even most importantly perhaps his opponents of the importance and futility of ever being on the side of that which is not and cannot be considered completely righteous.*

From my son Andrew Hanna:

Every young boy's dream is to be in the presence of a real-life hero, so from my earliest memories of learning that my father was a police officer, I was fascinated. I knew my dad was my hero. I knew that he went to work every day and kept the "good guys" safe and put the "bad guys" in jail.

Of course, everything I knew about the police came from reruns of "Chips" and "Adam 12," but I knew enough to know that there were good and bad in the world and the police? well, they were the good guys. But even at that young age, he was careful to explain to me that "bad guys" were often "good guys" that made poor choices and once they paid their debt to society, or got the help they needed, they'd have another chance.

I don't recall ever worrying about my father's safety in those days. I'm sure my parents had conversations with me about the dangers so obviously associated with police work, but I don't recall any of them. What I remember is having this sense of confidence in my father and knowing that he would come home at the end of the day. Looking back now, I think it was his stoic personality that relieved any fear I might have had and after all, I knew he had survived being shot at point-blank range and what could've been worse than that?

When I was old enough, I went to work with him on many occasions. As I watched him work, he'd answer my many questions and explain to me why he was doing what he did. I learned a lot from these experiences and I began to understand the type of police officer my father was. To him, police work didn't begin when a crime had occurred and end when a conviction was obtained. Rather, he believed in serving the community just as much as he believed in protecting it. He saw police work as a lifelong service to one's neighbors and that no life was worth giving up on. He helped organizations dedicated to preventing juvenile delinquency and he'd follow up with people he had arrested after they were released from prison. He'd speak with anyone willing to listen about the importance of making good choices and accepting accountability for one's own actions. To him, preventing a crime was more important than solving one.

There's hardly a day gone by in Madison County where someone hasn't recognized my name or relayed an anecdote or two about my father's career, and there's hardly a day gone by that I am not reminded of my father's impact on our community and the principles he stands for.

If I was looking for something to brag about in life I wouldn't have to look past my fine sons.

* * * * * *

2 Corinthians 12:9-10 says, *But he said to me, "My grace is sufficient for you, for my power is made perfect in weakness." Therefore I will boast all the more gladly about my weaknesses, so that Christ's power may rest on me. That is why, for Christ's sake, I delight in weaknesses, in insults, in hardships, in persecutions, in difficulties. For when I am weak, then I am strong.* (NIV)

If you read or watch the news on TV you could easily come to believe that our world today has gone crazy. As I have written about my career I wanted to bring to light what I faced as a police officer. In times of crisis, Christ's power rested on me and gave me the power to continue my job.

As children of God, we all experience times when we are confronted by our own weaknesses on a daily basis. It is because we are imperfect that mistakes are made every day. Teachers, police officers, parents, and religious leaders all can fall short of our expectations and when they do their mistakes have a negative effect on our families, friends, and neighbors. For our society to heal and become a safe place in which to raise our families we need the healing and restorative power of Christ.

Some Final Notes

Today, and when I first started on the police force, we often times find ourselves fighting an uphill battle. We need Christ's strength in order to be able to continue to protect and serve this country.

If we all served God and treated each other with respect and encouragement this would be a better world. This can be done in all walks of life, not just police work.

Again, I didn't write this book to brag about "the great Sam Hanna." If there is any greatness in me it is my great concern and respect for my fellow officers – especially the young officers who are just starting out. I wanted to share with others in my profession the good mentoring I received, my good and bad choices, and my partnership with God's grace and wisdom. These things guided me through my career and made my work successful. It can all be summed up in these thoughts:

It is not the gun or the vest that will save you in your work. It is the development of your principles and your character that will make you strong enough when you have to face life point blank.

House of Representatives

HONORING SAM HANNA ON THE
OCCASION OF HIS RETIREMENT

HON. MIKE PENCE
OF INDIANA
IN THE HOUSE OF REPRESENTATIVES
Wednesday, April 6, 2011

Mr. PENCE. Mr. Speaker, I rise today to honor the long and storied career of Sam Hanna. Sam is not only a friend, but a man whom I greatly admire.

Sam has strength of character and a true servant's heart in his community. After graduating from Anderson High school, he went on to receive a degree in Administration of Criminal Justice from Anderson University and then graduated from the Indiana Law Enforcement Academy. He is a member of the Madison Park Church of God, and coached football in the Anderson community for thirty years.

Never one to sit on the sidelines, Sam has boldly answered the call of duty even in the face of danger. In 1978 Sam was shot six times in the line of duty—in the face, chest, and arm. Yet even after that tragedy, Sam remained dedicated to public service and only recently retired after 37 years of service with the Madison County Sheriff's Department.

Those who know Sam and worked with him on the sheriff's department recognize him for his dedication to helping others and willingness to do whatever it takes. He served selflessly day after day, and received the distinguished "Law Enforcement Officer of the Year" award five times. I know that his integrity and commitment to the cause will forever be an example to those who serve after him.

Though Sam has officially retired from the Madison County Sheriff's Department, he continues to serve as Investigator of Senior Protective Services for the Prosecutor of Madison County. He is a dedicated husband of more than thirty years to his bride Lori, and the father of three sons—Kris, Matt, and Andrew.

Today I honor Sam's legacy of service, and wish to express my sincere gratitude for his leadership. I am grateful for his friendship and look forward to his continued community impact. He is truly an inspiration.

Made in the USA
Lexington, KY
17 March 2016